T0065102

INSIGHT PITCH

INSIGHT PITCH

MY LIFE AS A MAJOR LEAGUE CLOSER

BY SKIP LOCKWOOD

FOREWORD BY FERGIE JENKINS

SPORTS
PUBLISHING

Sports Publishing books may be purchased in bulk at special discounts for sales promotion, corporate gifts, fund-raising, or educational purposes. Special editions can also be created to specifications. For details, contact the Special Sales Department, Sports Publishing, 307 West 36th Street, 11th Floor, New York, NY 10018 or sportspubbooks@skyhorsepublishing.com.

Sports Publishing® is a registered trademark of Skyhorse Publishing, Inc.®, a Delaware corporation.

Visit our website at www.sportspubbooks.com.

10 9 8 7 6 5 4 3 2

Library of Congress Cataloging-in-Publication Data is available on file.

Cover design by Tom Lau
Cover photo courtesy of the New York Mets

ISBN: 978-1-68358-175-8
Ebook ISBN: 978-1-68358-176-5

Printed in the United States of America

Dedicated to my 101-year-old mother, Florence Lillian Lockwood, who followed her dreams as a young girl and danced with the original New York City Rockettes. Thanks for letting your seventeen-year-old son chase his own dreams.

TABLE OF CONTENTS

PRELUDE

The Magic of Baseball

As a very young boy I see things, magic things.
They come to me without warning, faster and clearer some days.
Images wash over me, but only last for a moment or two.
I wonder about them. They are cloudy and sometimes alluring.

Today, they are back again stronger than ever . . . chasing me . . .
  even calling me.
I look down and gasp.
Like I'm watching a movie, suddenly I'm in a Major League Base-
  ball uniform.
It's opening day . . . My chest fills with pride . . . The crowd is
  buzzing.
With a sense of wonder, I stride onto the field.
The green thick grass sticks to my new high tops.
The crowd fills me with excitement. They chant my name in
  unison.

INSIGHT PITCH

My chest heaves . . . My feet feel light . . . My breath quickens.
I smile and nod knowingly.
Sauntering to centerfield, I join all my baseball heroes: Speaker,
Mantle, and Williams.
They greet me warmly.

Two outs later, I scale the padding on the center field wall and
snag a liner, robbing Mays of extra bases.

Now it's my turn to bat.
The bases are loaded. The crowd holds its breath in anticipation.
I wrap my hands around an old stick I find lying on the ground
and suddenly it turns into a Major League bat.
I straddle a piece of chipped asphalt siding, turned into home
plate.

I heft the instrument and raise it to the ready position, taking
measure of its
Power and potential . . . swishing and pointing it menacingly in
the direction of the pitcher.
The ball is en route. I make a perfect swing and feel the solid
contact.
The bat sounds like a rifle shot as it echoes against the capacity
crowd.
I see the ball rise. It's a homer. My heart soars.

As I cross home plate, the manager, who looks like a poster from
my bedroom, shakes my hand and bends over to ask me to

pitch a few innings. I agree of course, smiling as humbly as the legendary George Herman must have done when he was asked to do the same thing.

I sense a pale of fear washing across the faces of the opposing team.

Brimming with confidence, I decide it's too easy and boring for the crowd just to throw my fastball in order to overpower the batters.

So, with a smirk on my face, I grip the ball inside my glove, pressing it higher

Into my fingers and away from the palm,

My fingers tighten over the leather.

I focus on my target, rotate forward, and pull down hard on the laces.

The ball takes off . . .

It arches towards home plate . . . It bridges the distance . . . part hope . . . part real . . . part magic.

FOREWORD

FOR ME, THE game of baseball was more than just two
teams keeping score. It was a game that transcended
generations and lifted the spirit of entire cities. On a professional level, the playing of the game demanded strength and
courage. It involved physical and mental toughness and day-
to-day commitment to preparation, all things that I stressed
throughout my Major League playing career.

Competing at the highest level is not just about winning.
It's about having the courage to face life's challenges and
opportunities, recognizing your capabilities, striving for
excellence, and leaving your heart out on the field. Winning
was the result. Skip Lockwood has been able to capture that
spirit in his new book: *Insight Pitch: My Life as a Major League
Closer.* The book begins and ends with the premise that, at
any level and in any profession, you need to be able to create vivid and real images of yourself competing and winning
before you succeed.

I've always believed that mental attitude and concentration are the keys to pitching. The great players in baseball will

tell you that preparation begins with what's going on in your head. Skip's new book shows you how professional athletes get their edge.

—**Fergie Jenkins HOF 1991**
Cy Young Award 1971
Canadian Baseball Hall of Fame 1987
MLB Baseball Hall of Fame 1991

INTRODUCTION

BEFORE WE GET into the insight, let me fill you in on the short version. In 1964, straight out of high school, I signed a baseball contract with Charlie O. Finley, owner of the Kansas City Athletics. Over the next eighteen years I fulfilled a little boy's dream of playing America's Game in parts of the next three decades, alongside Hall of Famers Catfish Hunter, Nolan Ryan, Tom Seaver, Carlton Fisk, Frank Robinson, Willie Mays, and Satchel Paige.

I played third base with the A's organization for a couple of seasons, but a combination of poor eyesight and military service derailed my batting career. I made a transformation and became one of only a handful of players to go successfully from the infield to the pitcher's mound. I was selected by the Seattle Pilots in the 1968 expansion draft and played with that team in 1969. I was used mostly as a starting pitcher by the Brewers and the Angels from 1970 to 1974 and was traded to the Yankees during the 1974 offseason, but I was released just prior to the start of the season. One phone call later, I hooked on with Charlie Finley again and, after some mid-night shenanigans, was sent to the AAA Tucson Toros under an assumed name. I liked the heat of the desert and my new role as closer. In July of that year, I was purchased by the Mets to bolster their bullpen.

In New York, I blossomed as a reliever. In less than 50 innings for the Mets, I struck out 61 batters, averaging 11.4 Ks every 9 innings. In 14 of my 24 appearances, I fanned three or more batters. Perhaps my greatest effort came in 1975's final game, pitching the Mets to a winning record overall and helping Mets starter Tom Seaver win his third Cy Young Award. In 1976, I also recorded 108 strikeouts in 94⅓ innings, becoming the first Mets relief pitcher ever to strike out over 100 batters in a single season.

My 1975 to 1979 seasons are some of the best of any Mets reliever. I pitched in 227 games for the Mets, all in relief, with 24 wins and 65 saves, posting a 2.80 ERA while striking out more than a batter an inning. I was voted as the team's Rolaids Relief award winner three consecutive years, and in 1992, I was voted by Mets fans as their all-time favorite right-handed reliever.

In 1980, I signed as the first-ever free agent with the Boston Red Sox, going 3-1 before giving way to a nagging shoulder injury. My final pitching statistics were: 420 appearances, 1,236 innings, 829 strikeouts, 69 saves, and a 3.55 ERA.

In the following pages, you will learn about events from throughout my life. Care has been taken to make the stories as accurate as possible. Though some quotations may be fictionalized, every effort has been made to maintain the spirit of the original statements.

CHAPTER 1
LITTLE LEAGUE TRYOUTS

THE FIRST AND last time I ever threw a baseball deliberately at someone's head was during Little League tryouts. In the small town of Norwood, Massachusetts, in 1955, as an innocent nine-year-old, I had no concept of the possible consequences, no idea about how I would feel or how others would react.

Later that afternoon, in recalling the event, some people said that the ball got away from me and I really didn't mean to hurt anyone. Others speculated that my catching partner must have been distracted and just wasn't looking. Still others would hold that it was just a mistake. Truth be told, I knew.

What registered in my adolescent brain was the recognition that, because of forces that were completely unknown to me, I possessed something other boys my age did not—a special gift, perhaps, something that would be envied in the years to come. It, whatever you call it, appeared in that very minute and survived well into my adulthood.

Looking back the discovery was not all that earthshaking, but it dawned on me that if I gripped the seams of a baseball a certain way, it would react in predictable ways. I also realized that I could create the velocity by bearing down on the tips of my fingers and pressing the seams as I released it. The spinning motions could bring life to the ball . . . velocity and movement that someday would rip the webbing off a major league catcher's mitt and weaken the knees of even seasoned major league batters. From this day forward I was aware that, in grasping the baseball and throwing it with purpose, I held in my hand a possession that was in equal parts powerful and dangerous.

As things often do, this revelation began with uncertainty. On this overcast spring day, Little League tryouts were proceeding in a chaotic manner. Boys of all ages, sizes, abilities, and attitudes nervously assembled along neighborhood lines on the patchwork field of grass and mud. They were wandering around in baggy shirts, asking questions like, "When is this going to start? When am I going to get a chance to hit?"

Some of the boys had already lost their caps and misplaced their new gloves. A few were aimlessly crowding into small groups in various parts of the field, bored because, for some, their parents had made them come. By now many just wanted to go home. One little boy, awkwardly shifting weight from one foot to the other, was trying to find a coach. He had to pee badly.

Anxiously waiting for the tryouts to get going too, I was trying hard to control my pent-up excitement about finally getting a chance to try out for Little League and play ball on an actual field. My eyes wandered to the outfield when a boy came over and asked to play catch with me. Recognizing him from school, I eagerly grabbed my ball and glove. Quickly it became clear that though we might have been in different classes in school, we were in different stratospheres concerning baseball. I flashed a glance at his hands as he passed me the baseball. They were the hands of a child, soft and small. He didn't have calluses on the tips of his fingers from throwing a thousand balls at the cellar wall with a target drawn on it like a batter's box. He probably hadn't played out all of last season's Red Sox victories over and over again, while inserting himself in the center of the batting and pitching action. Based on his demeanor, he didn't seem at all determined to become a big league player someday, to pitch in front of a sellout crowd on opening day. These were things I believed and could not hide. Standing about twenty feet away from me, like a rag mop with his arms lying limp against his side, he played with the enthusiasm of a marble statue and the concentration of a ten-year-old, which was exactly what he was.

What in the world is wrong with him? I thought to myself. *Doesn't he know that each and every toss carries its own message, each throw is a personal point of pride and, more importantly, each throw is an action deserving of focus and deliberateness?* I certainly did, and more importantly, I had been taught by my father to take pride in every action on the baseball field. After all, everything happens for a purpose.

He obviously wasn't the best player on the team last season and now he seemed content to accept his mediocrity. The whole process of playing toss with him was getting tedious. I looked around for another boy to play with. I knew that every day on a baseball field came with its own challenges and this one was no different. But what kind of challenge was playing fetch with a dog? He couldn't even catch my half-speed tosses. I started to think of something to spark a little excitement. I challenged myself to make my own magic, to try something different.

****

I wind up the same way as I had before, but this time I aim the pitch directly at his head. Actually, I aim it at the insignia on his new baseball cap and let it fly with a flick of the wrist, pushing the ball forward with a gleam in my eye.

As the ball leaves my hand, I twist the Little League-approved seams, like the knob of a door handle, putting less pressure on my forefinger and more on my swear finger.

Making this exact same motion a thousand times, in the basement of my house over the cold winter months, with the same twisting motion, the results varied. The majority of those throws in the cellar produced a small downward movement, but this particular baseball, as if on cue, starts out towards his face but abruptly alters its course traversing his new uniform shirt, which is by now in full retreat.

Even from twenty feet away, I can see the white part of his eyes beginning to expand. Fear washes over his face. He knows he is in trouble. He throws his hands up in the air defensively as if to swat it off, a tactic that proves inadequate.

It doesn't look like any other pitch I have ever thrown. In fact, it is a little bit slower than I would have liked, but it does have bite to it. In the years to come, I'll refer to a pitch like this as, "Uncle Charlie" or maybe, more respectfully, "Sir Charles."

The ball hits him in his right knee as he shields his head and eyes. He crumbles to the ground, grabbing his shin, and starts to cry. I'm frozen in time, transfixed. I am amazed at the toss and how it reacted—the shape it made, the path it took, and the speed that it traveled.

****

Everyone flowed over to him to see what had happened. They were visibly upset, and I obviously was in real trouble. My teammate was hurt. He had been deceived. In the years to come, I would come to understand that the indignity of some prepubescent experiences can last forever. The sadness that comes in the form of the embarrassment of being left out of a particular game because of your size or being left out because you're a girl or because you looked nerdy can linger for years. These wounds inflicted by team sports or, in this case, the missing of a baseball so badly during tryouts, could survive for years, in many cases leading to the counseling couch later in life.

****

My emotions are vacillating between elation and concern. Yes, I am upset that I deliberately targeted a ball that caused injury to someone else, but there is also a tinge of something else, approaching pride, that I can throw such a cool pitch. The hard calluses on my fingertips tingle.

An adult, one of the coaches, leans down to console me, think-ing I am upset. "Don't feel badly young man. I don't think you hurt him," he says. Frozen in place, I don't move a muscle. I don't dare. It would be terribly wrong to show any other emotion than sadness. I force a concerned face.

Another coach comes over and points authoritatively to the other side of the field where the tryout players are being audi-tioned. He motions for me to go over there and get away from the situation. I'm relieved to have somewhere else to go. As I walk away I can still see the complete horror in the little boy's face as the pitch approaches him. I also recall the arc of the ball, spin-ning and curving towards his leg. These images form a lasting impression.

****

The incident was over with one pitch. I arrived at the other side of the dusty field, dotted with weeds and dirt patches, adjusting my new cap so the emblem was square in the mid-dle, letting go of the angst from a moment ago and embracing the new flutter of excitement. My dad was still waiting in line, where I had left him fifteen minutes ago, to register me for the tryouts. Norwood might have been a small town, but it had a big-league way of assessing Little League talent.

Coaches split tryouts up into skill sections. There was a throwing station, a batting station, and a running contest. The coaches would evaluate the kids, giving everyone an equal chance, and play a game at the end of it all. All the kids wanted to do was play, get an at-bat, and run the bases.

Head tryout coach, local insurance agent, and lifetime Little League volunteer Garz Gugliatta was in charge of the festivities. He stood tall at 6-foot-2 in the days before poor posture and jelly donuts took their toll. He had on a sweatshirt with holes in the elbows and paint stains near the neck. Garz knew everyone in town. To me, Coach Gugliatta looked jovial and trustworthy, but my attention was drawn to his rigid square shoulders, where it looked like a hanger was still lodged in his sweatshirt. His fingers were yellow from years of smoking. Animated and convivial, he was thoroughly enjoying the morning. Garz had been in the Little League longer than anyone could remember. He managed, coached, took care of the field, and umpired when needed. Garz, in this part of the world, *was* youth baseball.

Garz stuck out his hand to shake. I reached out tentatively and shook, feeling the strength of his grip as his massive hand completely enveloped mine like a submarine sandwich bun around salami. I pressed back, and he looked at me quizzically. Looking down at my glove, Garz noticed that it was all broken in. "Hey man. Now that's a fine-looking glove you've got there," he said to me, winking at my father. He probably had little ice-breakers for each and every young man. I was pleased he noticed. I broke it in carefully and always slept with the glove next to my pillow.

Looking toward my father, but not making eye contact, he floated a trick question. "Did you guys just move into town?" They both knew that you had to be a town resident, living within the town borders and paying taxes to the town, to play in the league. Garz thought he knew everyone, but he didn't recognize us.

"We moved in late last summer, but I felt, at the time my son here . . ." my father patted my head, and I pushed his hand away, not wanting to be seen as a little boy. "I felt," he continued, "he was a little on the young side to play, and besides, he was recovering from a serious arm injury." Garz's eyes broke away and searched down, wondering which arm I had hurt and if it had left visible marks. "He's fine now," my father continued. "I hope he's good enough to make a team. It would be good for him to meet other kids and have someone to play with."

Continuing to scan my arms wordlessly, Garz tossed a large clipboard aside. The registration papers and birth certificates clattered to the ground. He reached into his pocket and unwrapped and stuck a Tootsie Roll Pop in his mouth. Satisfied that he had covered the fundamentals, the formalities were over. It was time to get down to brass tacks. Garz had, over the years, seen almost every boy in the school system, and he knew what he was looking for. The coaching staff had been carefully picked not only for their baseball knowledge but also for their way with the kids.

"Before anything else, let's see you throw," he said in a stage whisper. Garz stepped back a few paces like one would at the beginning of a duel, both of us facing each other. Garz put on an old catcher's mitt that was more broken down than broken in. It looked like it might have been a child's mitt, and he had trouble getting his meaty fingers into it. "Step back over there," he said and pointed to a line of chalk that had been drawn in the grass that morning to designate the throwing station. Garz insisted on personally "interviewing" everyone who registered for Little League, and playing soft toss with every boy on the field was one way of getting a gauge on their maturity and, quite frankly, their interest. He had years of experience and prided himself on being an excellent judge of talent, even in young players.

Then Garz made a mistake, stepping back about twenty-five feet, a distance predetermined by the coaches for throwing evaluations. But he was way too close. Then he made another mistake, when he said to me, "Let me see your best fastball, young man."

For me, the paced-off distance between us was similar to the distance in the cellar, from the "pitcher's rubber" on the cement floor to the cellar wall where the square strike zone was painted. I had thrown baseballs, tennis balls, ping-pong balls, and every kind of ball across that distance for over three years. Being very eager to please, I did indeed "let it fly."

In the same breath, my father tried to say something to Garz, by way of a warning, but it was too late. The ball made a slight hissing sound as it gobbled up big chunks of the crisp spring air. It crossed the distance between us in no time. It was gathering speed as it passed the other coaches, who were enrolling the other children behind fold-out tables and chairs. One coach heard something funny and looked up just in time to see a very unfamiliar scene. In a millisecond, Garz was on the ground. He had taken the ball off the left shoulder, his glove still down by his side. It was just a glancing shot, but it dropped him like a line of laundry. He laid there stunned.

"Whoa, man! Where did that come from?" were the words that came out of his mouth as he lay in the dirt, sitting on the seat of his pants. He didn't appear to be hurt really. He was speechless, incredulous, and shocked. I was a little upset too because, by hitting Garz in the shoulder area, I had missed my target by more than a foot. I had been taught that the target was the middle of the letter on the front of the jersey. I had practiced that precise target area for years with Dad on the front lawn.

For Garz, missing my target was probably a good thing, because a better-located pitch might have hit him square in the heart, not his shoulder. After all, he was playing catch indefensibly, too close to what would be a fastball that the newspaper would write about over the years, a fastball that would be good enough to warrant a parade through the center of town thirty years to the day.

Today, however, Garz was on the ground and getting up slowly. This particular beanball did not go unnoticed. A cluster of men gathered around to check on his condition. "Where did it get you?" asked one of the other coaches. "Where did it come from?" asked another. "Jesus, are you okay? What happened?"

They looked around thinking it had come from the outfield or from some other coach. They looked at each other. These questions, of course, had only one answer. "That young man right there threw it," and he pointed a finger at me. I wanted to crawl in a hole somewhere and hide.

The Little League tryouts resumed from this point with a few enhanced safety measures hurriedly put in place and a new atmosphere of caution. As it turned out, I made a team, the Yankees, and don't you know it my coach would be Garz himself. My baseball career was off and running.

My father, a neat buttoned-down man, was a civil kind of blue-collar guy. He was a sturdy man, proper and respectful in all manner of behavior. He was never very talkative, but when he did say something, you had better listen. Growing up, he delighted in playing catch with me in the front yard when he finally got home from work. I would use his shiny pocket protector as a target. He never played any participation sports himself. He was too small and too poor. He was also not aware of what was going to unfold during the next several years. We were both about to experience a major learning curve.

Looking at his face when the teams were announced at the end of tryouts, he seemed genuinely proud that I had been selected, but walking out to the car, he grabbed the scruff of my neck, applying pressure to make his point. He said, "Just what were you doing out there? Did you know that pitch was going to hit that boy? And just what were you thinking, hitting the coach like that?" All legitimate questions that I didn't know the answers to. I shrugged and grumbled something inaudible. With still more pressure he said, "Were you trying to hurt anyone?"

His face was turning red, and he seemed visibly upset by my behavior. Maybe I was in trouble. He turned me around to face him and continued, "I never want to see you try to embarrass anyone with the same uniform on again. Do you understand?" I forced another shrug and showed more of a hang-dog look. I was, however, curious about the words he had chosen, "with the same uniform." Before we reached the car, and well away from the field and the other parents, he bent down and whispered, "Where did that curveball come from?" I could see a slight smile and repressed mirth wash across his eyes.

****

As baseball unfolded for me over the next five decades, it was the playing of the game, the physical and the emotional capricious components both on and off the field, that consumed my life. It was an adventure, a journey, a job, a source of continuous trials, and many a sleepless night. It took unexpected twists and turns, at times resembling a circus of death-defying acts, other times more like a grand stage filled with odd proportions and strange contradictions. All in all, the choreography seemed pre-written, even pre-ordained, filled with high octane and timeless themes of virtuosity, perseverance, history, and purpose.

The edges of the game I decided to play as a very young boy were always new, always moving. They often bled together, leaving the margins between what was real and what was not indistinguishable. With much effort, baseball conceded to my constant boyish behavior and showed me new ways of thinking, new images of myself that gradually came into focus over time.

Segments of my career that seemed illusive came within my grasp. It was as if I breathed life into them once I believed in them. Images I was able to create in my mind became living breathing things which, individually and collectively, became my life; a new life in a sport filled with texture, meaning, and content.

Because of the enormous odds against a ten-year-old having any kind of professional career, especially a career that would last over parts of three decades, it would appear that baseball had chosen me rather than the other way around. Baseball captured my heart, and it seemed to enfold around me as I grew older with a leathery grasp that lasted well into adulthood and beyond. It became enormously complicated and simple at the same time. Baseball grew to become my hope. It enveloped me.

Long before free agency and salary arbitration, one-year contracts were the norm. Insecurity was commonplace. Players were purchased and/or released at the whim of management, playing for way less money than today's players do. Without the security of a long-term contract, I never knew how long my run would last. Invectives spoke inside my head, "Be flexible, be brave, and don't ever quit." All sounded much like my father's stern but patient voice.

With a modicum of resilience and larger dose of determination, I learned how to adapt to each change of scenery and every changing role. The fact that I was actually being paid to play a game I would have gladly played for free seemed just too much to comprehend. I never dreamed I would be sent down, brought up, traded, sold, and released so many times or imagined I would have to change positions to hang on to a role—from infield to outfield, from starting pitcher to closer.

From the emotional highs in the major leagues to the daily grind in the bush leagues, the basic game remains the same but the external trappings vary vastly. Baseball and I shared a tear as my black teammates were treated with indignities and denied basic rights in "White Only" gas stations in Birmingham, Iowa, in A Ball. We shared solidarity as I tried to convince my Milwaukee Brewers teammates to give up their salaries and take a stand against inequities in Baseball's Basic Agreement that denied fair compensation for veteran players and unfairly restricted players' movement from team to team. Baseball and I grew gray around the temples as a twinge in my right shoulder defied diagnosis and shortened my fastball and my career.

The game of baseball might be measured in inches, but it's performed on a landscape that encompasses thousands of miles—a game of measurements. My story largely covers the territory of sixty feet six inches between home plate and the pitcher's mound, but it's also spanned the distance from Portland, Oregon, to Milwaukee, Wisconsin—the distance I traveled in one remarkable day to pitch my first innings in an exhibition game against Hank Aaron and his Atlanta Braves.

My story has as its backstop the American culture through the revolutionary 1960s, the flower-powered 1970s, and the early disco-dominated 1980s. Despite having 20/400 vision, I was conscripted into the Vietnam-era National Guard.

In doing so, I completely lost my position in baseball, literally and figuratively. My personal fortunes rose and fell on the caprice of a fastball. Amidst strikes and lockouts, the baseball community continued to struggle with the same problems that faced all Americans at that time: contorted race relationships and freedoms denied.

Mine is a personal story. Overcoming obstacles was central to the script, as was my refusal to accept "no" for an answer. Though I loved my uniform as a little boy, I found myself loving it even more as an adult. I continued. I persevered. I hoped.

It seemed like I stood at the brink of disaster daily, changing positions from infield to outfield, from outfield to pitcher, from starting pitcher to closer, hanging on to childhood exuberance in a game that demands grown-up grit. As it turned out, I lived out every little boy's fantasy. I shared a locker with Satchel Paige and with Hall of Famers like Luke Appling, Catfish Hunter, Nolan Ryan, Tom Seaver, and Willie Mays.

Thinking back over my eighteen-year career, the one thing that made the difference was the magic in the game itself. I was able to visualize a little boy stepping onto the field of his dreams and the magic of that action. Day in and day out, I could only go as far as my imagination would take me.

CHAPTER 2

NEW YORK METS RUBBER GAME, SEPTEMBER 28, 1975

AT THE END of September 1975, the New York Mets' once promising season was skidding to an 82-80 close. A team of game-weary men had battled like gladiators to capture the pennant but, in the end, yielded to a third-place finish in the National League's Eastern Division. For the most part, all had been decided and all had been written by the time the Mets pulled into Veterans Stadium to play the final weekend series with the Phillies, but personal pride, along with league-leading records, were still on the line.

This series would be the last start for several pitchers bidding to cap off good seasons. The first game on Friday belonged to Jerry Koosman, a veteran of the season's grind. He's what the players called "a gamer." His eleven-inning winning performance demonstrated an extraordinary combination of pitching prowess and tenacity. Jerry was not overpowering, but he got the Phillies out with good command of the strike zone and a sharp breaking ball that bit like a snake. All day batters found themselves fishing for pitches in the dirt before Jerry reeled them in with a strike.

The last series of the year was usually a lackluster affair, but this would be different. It was the end of a marathon, but the race was close, and both teams registered that it was time to shift all efforts to another gear. A lopsided loss on Saturday sent a parade of already punch-drunk pitchers into the contest for one more drubbing. Many were absorbing body blows like an arm-weary fighter. Round one went to the visitors, round two to the home team. The Mets' last game of the season would not only be the rubber game of the series but of extraordinary importance to one Tom Seaver.

The baseball season is comprised of 162 games, each with its own pressure. In the end, each individual game is just as important as any other, but certain games feel different because of the significance of the outcome. That day's game would likely be the determining factor in who would win the National League Cy Young award for 1975. And to make things more stressful, I was most likely going to play a major role in the action.

As the season had unfolded over the previous months, I'd worked my way into the role of "short man" or, as the newspapers have coined the term, the "closer." With Tom's prestigious award hanging in the balance, I would most likely be in the game as soon as the fifth inning, providing we had a lead. I knew this in advance. The coaches nodded at me when I got to the ballpark and players did much the same. The physical and emotional strain of being the closer in the middle of a close National League pennant chase had brought me close to exhaustion and exhilaration.

We arrived on the team bus, filed out, and walked down a long cement hallway filled with electrical cables on the floor and large vents overhead. Arriving at a door that said "visitors," we edged past an uninterested security guard reading the horse-racing sheet. Jim, a longtime guard, smiled a fatherly smile to everyone as they passed.

A few steps later and we were inside another world. Although that day, since it was the last game of the season, the locker room looked more like a storage container piled high with boxes, luggage, and baseball gear. The room was spacious, but far from cushy. Four-foot-wide wooden lockers faced each other and twenty feet in between a few leather lounge chairs had been placed in informal groups, along with a couch, across from a television. The interior of this clubhouse had seen its share of frustrations this season. It's been said that you can tell where the home team finishes by the condition of the water cooler in the visiting club house.

In my career, there had been crazy antics and outrageous behaviors exhibited in the locker room. Once in a game against the Milwaukee Brewers, a player angry at being lifted for a pinch hitter in the ninth inning went up to the showers and turned them off by hand. Later, when the game ended, no one could turn them back on, and we all had to shower back at the hotel.

NEW YORK METS RUBBER GAME, SEPTEMBER 28, 1975

I had come to grips with the fact that the Mets were not going to win a pennant that year, so all the pressure should have been off. Nevertheless, we were still playing for pride.

****

As a journeyman pitcher I had, over the years, learned to live with the pressure of the do-or-die games. This was going to be one. What I also learned was not to run away from the pressure. Don't try to hide or pretend that it doesn't exist. If you do, it will find you, and you'll be unprepared.

Before each game, I'd get ready mentally. I prepared for every pitch and every possible outcome before it happens. I'd been practicing what some call mental imagery for most of my career. I called it focus, enhanced focus, intense concentration. It was never the same meditative state, and on that day, with all the confusion in the clubhouse, it would be even harder. There were twenty newspaper reporters milling around. There was a game show blaring on a gigantic television in the middle of the room.

Before I went onto the mound in a situation where I had to succeed, I needed to feel all the feelings first, conquer all the demons, and get a crystal-clear image of exactly what it would look like to win.

Winning baseball is all about control.

Usually, I'd hide in the trainer's room or a broom closet, somewhere quiet. I'd elevate my feet and start to go over the events of the upcoming game in vivid detail. Meditating and visualizing had become a part of my pregame routine, as much a part of the uniform as the hat or the belt. It's hard to know where reality begins and ends.

Lying on my back, fully dressed in my uniform from my cleats to my hat, at a distance of about twelve inches from the wall, I gently put my feet on the white painted cinder blocks, as to not make a mark I have to clean later. There was a ball in my right hand, and that was one of the keys. It connects me to the game, the game I'd be in the middle of in a few hours. I closed my eyes . . . take a few deep slow breaths. I knew if I could control my breathing in that moment I could manage it later, on the mound, when it counted.

The things I saw were exactly the situations I'd face on the field. I needed to reproduce the pressure, the heart-pounding compression in my chest and the feeling of nausea in my throat. Over the years I'd become acutely aware that you have to run toward the anxiety. This anxiety was my daily companion. I'd wait for it, and I'd know it must be stopped and controlled before I stepped on the field.

****

Slowly breathing in . . . I exercise control. I'm reducing my heart rate.

Slowly exhaling deeply . . . I picture blowing away all my bad thoughts.

I see myself on the mound, like watching a film.

I'm pitching an inning to a right-handed batter. I bend for the sign.

Things are happening slowly, deliberately . . . just as planned. I am an observer . . . a movie director, a third party. I watch the pitches, one by one. The throws arc towards the catcher. I hear the catcher's mitt crack as the ball makes a small amount of smoke come out of it. I shift my attention to the batter. His eyes are surprised. He is motionless. His bat is extended and then withdrawn.

I refocus now to being inside my own skin, seeing everything with my own eyes.

Regripping the ball in my hand, I enjoy the feeling of dominance and control.

I say out loud, "This pitch is for you." I feel the wind blowing the air between us . . . it's cool. I can hear the roar of the crowd like I'm standing next to the ocean.

Raising the glove to the bridge of my nose, I get a sign. The glove is another tool. It blocks out everything but the batter and the catcher. I lock in. My back foot digs a little bit at the mound like a horse at the starting gate.

The ball is in the glove, not because I want to hide it. It's staying warm. I say out loud, "You'll see it soon enough."

I feel the heaviness from thousands of eyes. My heart jumps. I take another deep breath, hold it, and let it go . . . very slowly. I spin the ball a little and grip it across the seams. The seams are tight and tough. They chafe against my fingers.

I dominate the ball. I want it to feel small in my hand . . . obedient to even the most subtle pressure. The distance between the mound and home plate is a space that I will shorten. I draw the hitter towards me. I reel him in like a fish.

I'm very calm, and I'm in control of my breathing. I look toward the catcher for the signs . . . but they're irrelevant. We agree on the pitch. He moves to the inside part of the plate. It's a heater . . .

a smoker. You'll hear it coming before you see it. It cracks like a whip. It has a life of its own.

I start into my windup, but really, I just get the ball started. I pull the trigger, and it comes out hunting . . . looking for a weakness and creating vulnerability. It's got your name on it.

I picture the look on the batter's face, the timidity in his swing. The pitch is a little more than he thinks . . . more than he expects. It zooms past before he can react . . . it gulps up the distance like a hungry snake.

Getting the ball back from the catcher, I snatch it out of the air, taking a step toward the batter. I glare at him menacingly, "Don't look down." I say out loud. "Look at me."

This is between you and me. It is very personal. Fuck all these people. "Do you what to know what's coming next? More of the same or maybe something with a bend to it." I picture the ball bending as sharp as a knife edge. I see his knees give way. I ready for the second pitch. He understands things much better now. I own this space between us, and the best he can do is try to save face. I stare in for a sign.

As my meditative session draws to a close, I loosen the seams of the ball slightly. Then I squeeze it again and then loosen. My deliberate thoughts shift to inside my own head. My mind goes to the ball in my hand. It feels like a gun that is still loaded. I feel the total control that I can execute the pitch, like shooting down a gun barrel. I control the time. I'm ready to go when the batter's foot hits the batter's box, and that's when I'm going.

Meditation is over. I have a greater sense of control, a heightened ability to focus and more importantly enhanced clarity and *vision. The taste in my mouth is sweet. It only takes about twenty minutes to prepare the game. I feel calm, prepared. I am not blocking any negative thoughts or emotions or trying to cover them up. I let them flow naturally. They are all part of the plan today. I will succeed because of the negatives and my ability to turn them into a great performance.*

During the day, the baseball will be my anchor. It will remind me of who is in charge, and it gives me tactile strategy. I lower my feet to the side slowly. I'm ready for the real game, the real pressure, and the real fear.

****

The last game of the year was a back and forth contest, as expected, for the first several innings. Dave Kingman, leading off the fifth, swung for the World Trade Center and hit a dying quail down the right-field line for a double. He slid into second looking like a ballerina in a batting helmet. Ed Kranepool fouled the first pitch off into the stands, sending a wave of flurry through the crowd as young kids battled middle-agers with beers in their hands for the souvenir. Seaver was a craftsman. His curve was sharp. It daggered the inside corner on Bob Boone, who returned with resignation to the dugout.

Seaver entered the sixth inning with a 5-1 lead. He walked Tom Hutton and Jay Johnston to start the sixth inning. Mike Schmidt laid down what was projected to be a perfect sacrifice bunt to third base and ended up getting a single. The bases were loaded. The phone rang in the bullpen. Joe Pignatano, the bullpen coach, picked the handle up like a barbell.

His eyes scanned the bench beside him. He stopped at me as he spoke with Rube Walker on the bench. He pointed and uttered two words, "Get up." He made a motion with his fingers to make it snappy. Feeling a rush of energy, I grabbed my old leather glove with the crossed-out numbers on the back flap and scrambled out of my Mets warmup jacket. I missed the bench as I ran to the warmup mounds, and the jacket fell in the tobacco seeds puddle in front of Bob Myrick.

The first throw was short in distance but had nice carry on it. It snapped the strings in the catcher's mitt. John Stearns pointed the glove at me, acknowledging the velocity. Roy McMillan, the Mets manager, was out on the mound talking to Seaver. The conversation dragged on. He was taking his time, walking slowly, talking in his southern drawl, pointing to the infielders to make them aware of the double play combinations and responsibilities. The meeting ended. Seaver looked tired. I threw my fifth and sixth warmups. Piggy said, "Are you anywhere like close?" Without looking at him, I answered, "I'm ready." I was really not "ready," but I sensed that the ball had enough life to it that I could be ready before I faced a hitter. "I'll get a few more throws out there." Piggy looked doubtful, but took his hat off, the bullpen signal that "he's ready." Mike Rogodzinski singled to right, scoring Hutton and Johnston.

McMillan, having just reached the bottom step of the dugout, turned on a dime to retrace his tracks to the mound. It's his second trip, so he would have to make a change. The last afternoon shards of light were turning Veterans Stadium into an autumnal kaleidoscope. The shadows were lengthening around home plate. Seaver waited for Roy to climb the hill and handed him the ball definitively. Unbeknownst to me, the decision as to which pitcher to bring in and when to bring him in had been thoroughly discussed before the game.

The National League poster boy was leaving the game. But there was no apology in Seaver's demeanor. With or without this win, he would probably capture his third Cy Young award, but he wanted the win. The people in Veterans Stadium were baseball fans. They acknowledged Tom's talent with thunderous applause. An old man in the front row, surrounded by empty beer containers, vilified Seaver for being a Met and then for not finishing the Phillies off.

Seaver was arguably one of the best pitchers in baseball history, but on that day he faced some slower steps in his search to make history. All year he had been a filament in the white-hot globe of New York. He lit the way for the Mets, adding structure and dignity to a game played with joyful abandon by the Lost Boys of Neverland. He offered grace to a game of dirt and pine-tarred hands and thoughtfulness to a physical game. But being the best pitcher in the National League can be a strain on one's humanity. The cost of being responsible for a magician's act all season had strained the lids of his eyes and slumped his shoulders. Today, as the late afternoon sun filtered through the infield, that light shone just a little dimmer.

****

I'm entering a close game with a man on third, nobody out, tying run at the plate. I feel the anxiety building up in my stomach.

INSIGHT PITCH

It flutters, threatening. I know enough to expect that feeling, encourage it. I won't even try to block it. The way through the feeling is to build success one action at a time. To take command of it, to use it, to come after the batter harder, faster.

****

Before I arrived in New York, I would try to hide from my emotions, overcome them, and swallow harder. Tom Seaver took a different approach. He was a big advocate of being prepared to pitch, mentally and physically, so you could go to the mound and feel free to succeed.

Psychologically, there's a tipping point to this game. There is no such thing as a meaningless throw. Every pitch carries a message, a purpose. The psychology of pitching revolves around concentration, which translates into control—being able to gain the upper hand by being in better control, by having better focus. It's not trying to outguess the batter or coming up with a weird assortment of pitches. It's being in control of what you are thinking, and that manifests itself into the pressure of your fingers on the ball. Pitching is an extension of your personality, an exponent of emotion and determination. It's not pitching to the hitter's weakness; it's pitching to your strength. Control means getting the upper edge and keeping it.

Pitching inside is an acquired skill. For the previous two months before that September game, I had been studying and learning. The inside part of home plate has a black edge on it. On that day, that black edge would be mine. It was the sixth inning—the baseball equivalent of no man's land. The game was far from over. On the home side of the field optimism was running high. All the Phillies were on the front railing of the dugout clapping, pounding fists full of air. In relief I would have to turn the batting order over twice. Philly fanatics were smelling blood.

Over the years I would come to realize that I had more control over unexpected circumstances than I originally thought. Practice would turn into a profession. Hopes would turn into reality. Heroes would turn into teammates. Caution would turn into daring, and a young boy who wore very thick glasses would find, in a game, a world that would never leave him far from the field or the colorful people on it.

You might wonder how in the world a player can handle this "New York State of Mind" pressure. The answer is the same as the response to that age-old question, "How do you get to Carnegie Hall?—practice, practice, practice . . . . and leave all your baggage behind."

CHAPTER 3
THE DISABLED LIST, JULY 1952

IT STARTED OUT as a normal visit to my mother's sister's house, although it promised to be a scorcher. Aunt Peg, the oldest of a family of eight, had the best old thread-barren sofa perched against the back porch, the kind of couch that spurred on a six-year-old kid's imagination. Today I would be riding that couch like a bucking bronco for Teddy Roosevelt's Rough Riders, going after Pancho Villa down on the Mexico border like my great-grandfather Claude Silver Lockwood. Galloping hard on the arm of the sofa, I lost my balance, snagged my foot in between the seat cushions, and crashed through a window that divided the porch from one of the tiny bedrooms. The sound of shattered glass could be heard all through the house. I felt something sharp against muscles, tendons, and ultimately the bones of my right elbow.

My father arrived at the ICU in a frenzy but was forced to pace the halls for what seemed like hours while I was in surgery. His mind was spinning. He was running on nervous energy and fighting back waves of nausea. He was well past tears and close to exhaustion. This whole thing was just taking too long. He was waiting for some hope from the head of the emergency surgery team that had been hastily assembled earlier this morning.

"Claude," someone said loudly. From his slumped dead-tired position in the claustrophobic waiting room, he bolted to attention. The man calling his name was dressed head to foot in green pajamas with a matching surgical mask that had been pulled aside. There was a sense of resignation in his demeanor and frustration on his face. He looked exhausted. A green bandana sagged over his mouth and chin, and a stained apron covered his scrubs. My father's throat constricted as the two made eye contact.

"Mr. Lockwood," he began with measured words. "I am Henry Putnam, the lead surgeon on your son's case. I'm sorry it took so long to get out here and give you an update. Can we please sit down?" My father knew instinctively that sitting wasn't a good sign.

The doctor spoke deliberately, well-practiced at picking just the right common words for complex cases. "Your son has suffered lacerations caused by a jagged piece of irregular glass, which has torn the soft tissue on the inside of his right arm on the opposite side of the elbow. He has suffered heavy bleeding, which we have completely controlled. We are in the final process of interior and exterior sutures, and he will be fitted with a sterile cast for support. He will have to keep the arm elevated for a couple of days and will have to keep the bandage on and the wound clean."

He slowed his speech down as he reached the important part. The words dripped out, "He has had a lot of trauma to the bone and the tissues around the right arm for a boy his age. In plain English, he has a deep-cut wound to his right inner arm just opposite the elbow. The sharp edge of the window glass he fell through almost completely severed his right arm." He paused again.

"The good news is, we were able to reattach everything." The words "bone" and "reattach" slapped my father in the face. "It is tough to say at this early stage what the long-term effects of his accident today will be. Time will tell." He hesitated, "It's a very good thing he didn't fall all the way through the glass or we could be talking about much more serious injuries." Then his face brightened as if he had thought of something positive he missed and said reflectively, "In many respects, your son's a lucky young man, although it may not seem that way now, and I expect to see him in a Red Sox uniform someday."

The absurdity of his words hung in the air a few moments, almost patronizing given the situation. He undoubtedly had used this line before. Dad's face brightened to match the doctor's expression, an automatic reaction. He was clinging to anything hopeful at this point. Dr. Putnam was gone as quickly as he arrived. Dad was left with his feelings, powerless to move or think. The words "completely severed" were ringing in his ears. His eyes watered and every muscle in his body ached.

In that instant he made a commitment to himself and to his son. If baseball is the essence of hope, then playing baseball would be the core of his son's recovery. He was determined to be his Little League coach, even though he knew very little about the game. He would rethink his work and especially the commute. Already devising a rehabilitation plan, he yelled down the empty hallway, "You better believe he'll be in a Boston uniform someday."

A few hours later, Dad was at Sears & Roebuck searching for the sports equipment department. He wandered until he was standing in front of the baseball gloves. Coming from a very small town he knew little or nothing about baseball or baseball gloves. This was the first baseball glove he ever purchased, and he didn't know what he was looking for. He wasn't even sure if he should purchase a right- or left-handed glove. The gloves were scattered on the shelf.

He decided to buy himself a catcher's mitt because it looked like it had lots of padding. He snagged two baseballs displayed next to the gloves and noticed that they were Little League-approved. He wondered whether I would ever get to wear a Little League uniform. He pictured my deformed chicken-like wing in the sleeves of a Little League jersey. Shaking that painful thought out of his head, he continued to check out.

I might have plunged into the world of baseball because of a lame limb, but once caught up in the game, I was hooked for life. As soon as the external wounds healed it was time to work on strengthening the internal damage. When Dad got home from work, a ritual unfolded. He would loosen his tie and take out his plastic pocket protector, careful not to disturb the order of the contents. Therapy turned into fun, though initially I'd be battered by a range of questions and directives.

"How are you feeling today?"

"Let me see the scar."

"Wow that really looks good, does it still hurt?"

A shrug of the shoulder meant no discernible change from yesterday when it was okay. No other words were necessary. We separated ten feet, then fifteen, and the ball flew, but more often bounced, between us. Dad never said anything but "nice throw" over and over again, even when the ball didn't have enough steam to make it halfway to his glove. "I'll get it," he would say. "Stay right there and get ready for the heater again."

The intention was clear. Two gloves and a ball were the prime ingredients in an alchemy of hope and recovery. The journey began and, once underway, turning back was never an option. The expectation was always to do better than the day before. Simple, take small steps. Take joy in feeling better. We started playing catch in the front yard, then moved to the back. My arm strengthened over the summer, and the pain from the glass began to fade. Within a week or two we went from playing fetch to playing catch—tentatively but catch nevertheless. Playing catch became the bond between us, sacrosanct. It provided hope in small doses. Dreams started to sprout for each of us and, out of the vestiges of a disaster, something began to take its place.

Summer lingered, but the days started to grow shorter. My father couldn't always get home in time with enough daylight for a suitable game of catch. So one weekend we devised a makeshift workout center in our cellar. That winter

I continued to throw every day in the cement and cinder-block-lined hole under the kitchen stairs known as the basement. I was very focused for a six-year-old. Night after night I peppered that square in the basement with tennis balls. From upstairs, my parents were serenaded by a symphony of rubber striking cement.

In the spring of my seventh year, a whole new world opened up for me. I discovered my yard was filled with pebbles. This was a goldmine of ammunition. At first, I raked the rocks into piles and built a rocky fortress but, as an only child, there was no one against whom I could defend this fort. Then I started tossing the stones up in the air and swinging at them with a broomstick. This was a lot more fun. Soon I traded in my broomstick for a small wooden bat. I got pretty good at whacking the rocks into the woods about twenty feet away. I liked the sound the rocks made when they hit a tree. After I got pretty good at hitting the stationary trees, I started aiming at the squirrels who ran past. Now I had moving targets. Every day I practiced with fanciful tunnel vision.

CHAPTER 4

WELCOME TO SHEA STADIUM, 1975

FROM THE FIRST base dugout, Yogi Berra yelled, "Come on Chip, throw strikes." His husky, hoarse voice, distinguishable above the din of the Shea Stadium crowd, bellowed: "Come on Chip, get this fucking batter out."

Breezes off the Flushing Bay usually whipped the hot dog wrappers into mustard and ketchup tornadoes along the third base line this time of night, but not today. Today the air was still, except for the swoosh and swipes of the Expos' bats at Mets pitching, ash wood thrusting, balls and bat ricocheting like gunshots. It was mid-summer and the New York Mets, in the middle of the National League East pennant race, were struggling with their late-inning relief pitching. They were in desperate need of a reliever who could hold a lead or at least stay close enough after a slugger like Eddie Kranepool or John Milner took one deep to right. For the Mets, replacing their bullpen ace, the "Ya Gotta Believe" closer extraordinaire Tug McGraw, proved more difficult than anticipated.

Rumors of discontent ran rampant, arguments in the locker room spilling into the manager's office. Yogi Berra's stoic facial expression belied his desperate demeanor. The players could hear it in his voice. The press might cut him some slack because, after all, he was Yogi, famous for his unbridled determination and confounding comments. But his bellowing rang hollow those days as the Mets trampled through relief pitchers. Berra coached the Mets for seven roller-coaster seasons, including their miraculous 1969 World Championship, and was in his fourth season as Mets manager. Always an optimist, he's perhaps known best for his Yogi-ism, "It ain't over till it's over." Today's game wasn't over either, by any stretch of the imagination, but when stalwart Jerry Koosman unexpectedly ran into trouble in the third inning, it was time to change pitchers. Yogi ambled to the pitcher's mound, taking his time, giving the pitcher a few extra throws. Yogi signaled to the bullpen, tapping his right sleeve to bring in a newcomer who had just arrived a few hours ago—me. After the umpire gave his signal, I was ready and on my way in—a little more than duct tape on an expensive franchise leaking oil.

Bringing in a recently arrived, unknown pitcher, especially one from outside the organization, can be risky. For one thing, the newcomer doesn't know the hitters. He doesn't know his own team's defensive alignment. He doesn't know the signs. He doesn't know the culture. Despite all these negatives, Yogi felt it was a reasonable gamble given the current state of the bullpen.

The humidity was holding in the 90 percent range and the patience of the Flushing Meadows season ticket holders was running thin. Yogi waited on the mound, round-shouldered, impervious, ready to hand me the baseball. He was joined by the infielders, a retinue with important issues to discuss.

I arrived on the mound. Yogi said, "There's two guys on. I don't think they're going to fucking bunt with this kind of a lead, but you don't know. You need to throw strikes and get your ass over to the line if Foote lays one down. Go get him Chip."

Not waiting for a reply, Yogi stepped off the mound embankment and headed for the shelter of the Mets dugout as the fans rained down their displeasure. One disgruntled fan aimed an invective in his direction, "Can't you find anyone who even looks like a ballplayer?" Once back to the dugout, he spat a dark stream at the corner puddle, turned back towards the field, and shouted an expostulation: "Come on Chip. Let's go. Throw strikes. Shit."

****

Yogi's invectives are aimed at me. I am standing on the Shea Stadium pitcher's mound for the first time, about to throw my first pitch in the 1975 National League Pennant Race. I paw the red clay on Shea's pitcher's mound dug into several sizable craters created by Koosman's cleats. Sweat drips off the back of my neck. My heart pushes against the blue-and-orange lettering on my shirt. I need to collect myself. Warmup pitches will help.

If it looks like I am stalling for time, I am. Well-worn words form in my mouth, "Concentrate, collect yourself." I recite the mantra out loud, behind the mound. Another acclamation, "Come on Chip. Let's go. Throw strikes," surfs towards me over the roar of the capacity crowd.

I hear Yogi, but I can't see him. In hot sticky situations my glasses always steam up like a shower mirror. Professional athletes don't usually wear glasses and, for sure, Big League Baseball pitchers rarely wear glasses. These lenses are, indeed, no ordinary eyewear. These lenses are designed to prevent bumping into walls. These lenses are industrial-strength plastic, about a centimeter at the extremities. They might have been issued by the Defense Department for repelling bullets. They can survive a nuclear bomb. But because of the thickness of the lenses they have a tendency to sweat-up with body heat and are presently juiced up by the late August barometer in New York and the pressure of the situation. Glasses in one hand, a new National League baseball in the other, and my glove cradled under my left arm, the lenses appear to be clearing up. The delay in the action on the field is causing the crowd to grow restless, a similar effect that it has on the Montreal Expo batter, Barry Foote, and the Mets catcher, John Stearns, whose name at this point in time I can't remember. It is also causing the umpire, Satch Davidson, to walk towards me.

"Come on. Come on. Just clear up." I counsel the lenses, sensing the urgency of the moment. I pull the damp leather strap on my glove with my teeth, tasting the salty sinew. From the dugout Yogi yells again, "Come on, Chip. Let's pick up the pace."

I can't wait any longer. I roll the expandable sports temples around my ears, looking more like John Lennon than Johnny Baseball.

With glasses affixed I glance out towards the visiting Montreal Expos' bullpen, beyond the left field fence. The inhabitants of said bullpen are behaving very strangely—all standing, noses pressed to the outfield fence, clapping in unison, cheering for me. Some are laughing, others are banging on the Plexiglas partisan in the left field fence—a strange scene playing out in professional sports.

****

Just to set the record straight, my name is not Chip, but I don't blame Yogi for the mistake. He and I met on the pitcher's mound for the first time, and it was very noisy. He was distracted. And I played for the New York Mets, not the Montreal Expos. The reason as to why the Expos bullpen acted like a bunch of monkeys will force me to recount a rather embarrassing story.

It's the fifth day of August 1975, midway through my summer of destiny. Traveling to Shea Stadium with a purpose, I shared a first-class cabin on Piedmont Airlines out of Charlotte with an elderly couple who spoke in stage whispers, folding and refolding Tour Guide maps. The couple appeared to be on a marriage renewal, celebrating years of devotion, infidelities released long ago, financial insolvencies resolved by well-paid counsel, offering them a second chance. I was hoping for a second chance too—or third or fourth—a chance to take another swing at a little boy's game, a game in which I'd been privileged to play different roles in different arenas all across this country. My journey was not listed in any tour book.

I closed my eyes and flashed to a silhouette of a ball field outlined against the desert sands. Monochromatic. Stark. Simple. A tintype photo. It's the last game I pitched in Tucson, Arizona, AAA League. It's only two days ago, but already it seems out of focus.

****

I'm throwing a fastball to a lefty.

My lead toe drags and scrapes on the dusty chipped pitcher's mound.

The fastball paralyzes my opponent. He doesn't even offer at it. He can't. The ball is coming on a straight path, with no arc, but maybe a slight rise.

I throw it with a swift, angry motion and a determined expression. Breaking free from my hand, the ball bites at the hot desert air, first searing the inside corner of home plate and then skating the outside corner.

He's overpowered and lowers the bat.

My Tucson Toros catcher, Charlie Sands, signals another heater. I can see the defiant one-finger sign, a toothy grin behind the mask.

The ball's en route. Charlie growls, "See ya," as the batter tries to level his shoulders to get his bat on the plane, but he's too late by a wide margin. He swings, but the ball is already in the mitt. The fastball in the dry desert heat has come alive.

The pitches are reacting like a whip—starting out rather slow, laying out towards the target, and then unfurling, a blur past the batter.

I hear it pop against Charlie's leather mitt again and again. I revel in the sound. He's resorted to using a falsie inside the mitt to protect his hand.

****

Staring out the plane window, fifteen hundred miles away from the ballpark in Arizona, my hand was twitching. I felt the tingles in the tips of my fingers like the trigger of a gun. The pitch of the plane pulled me back.

From Tucson AAA in the Pacific Coast League to New York City, home of the New York Metropolitan National League franchise, I traveled light. I carried a vintage Samsonite hand-me-down, covered with logos and duct tape on one edge, packed with a few shirts inside, wrinkled by now and more suited for correcting term papers than pitch count. My baseball duffel, navy blue with the name Brewers stenciled in orange on the outside, was missing a few letters. My name, written in marker on adhesive tape underneath, was barely visible. Inside were two gloves, a lucky and very holey T-shirt, a worn down pair of sneakers with the Arizona red clay still clinging to the grooves, and a black pair of Rawlings baseball spikes, re-tied above one of the eyelets. The tattered tongue, sticking out with crossed out Magic Marker numbers, appeared to be mouthing stories from baseball fields in big cities and small towns all across the country. Together and separately they were vestiges of a well-traveled career.

My looks were unremarkable. I was six feet tall, with longish brown hair and a hint of gray near the temples, balding at the crown. Athletic compared to the general population, I was clothed in a blue golf shirt, jeans, and heavy tortoiseshell glasses, not so cleverly disguised as sunglasses, covering a round tanned face, "sun-stained with mileage" as the saying goes. My large paddle-shaped hands were marked with protruding veins. Hard calluses could be found at the first and second fingertips on my right hand. A large scar, roughly the size and shape of Texas, decorated the inside of my right arm. My left hand was in better condition covered with a gold-black strapped watch, a high school graduation gift from my mother two days before I left home at the age of seventeen. The watch was set for Arizona time.

At twenty-eight-years-old I was, in the parlance of baseball, a journeyman—a pitcher with good stuff, an overly intense mound demeanor, and completely no idea where home plate was, especially when the innings piled up and the bases were jammed with runners. The *Milwaukee Sentinel* wrote, "He's got more heat than Julia Child, but he can't find the plates, and lately, it looks like he is spending too much time in the kitchen." The truth about untapped talent echoed in the empty ballparks of a middle-market team like the Milwaukee Brewers, twenty games out of first at the All-Star break. I was hanging on to a career with grit and determination, but I knew I could not continue to trapeze between promises and pardons much longer. I openly wished for a new team one night in a crowded bar conversation with my Brewers pitching coach, Wes Stock. He cautioned me, "Be careful what you wish for."

The 1975 season had started out with a form letter. It stated that the New York Yankees had acquired me from the California Angels, where I had played the season before. Truth be told, I had rarely played. Instead of starting with the star-crossed Angels, I was banished to their bullpen in a season of unanticipated obscurity. The Southern California brass showed blatant indifference to giving this Northern New Englander another one-year contract for fourteen thousand dollars.

The previous night's sleep refused to come. Today's plane ride lulled me to doze in and out of a recurring dream. In it, I am a small boy, not only in size but in the sense of helplessness and vulnerability—at times indefensible, unable to make an audible sound despite being in great peril, chased and almost captured, barely escaping. I possess small feet, terrible for running through dense wet sand. I'm trying to avoid a demon, my mouth is wide-open, but no sound escapes. The plane jerked me back to reality. A cold wind rushing through the cabin sent a ripple through the fluttering head napkins. The flight was more than a little bumpy. My empty stomach churned slowly as the flight tumbled on. I was glad I had refused the meal and the beer cart offerings.

I tried to remain calm despite the distractions. I might have to work tonight, and that would require a clear mind and razor-sharp reflexes. Although my appearance would allow me to blend easily into a town this size, my purpose for being in New York City was anything but ordinary. I was heading to the Big Apple to perform what some would call a high-wire act—dangerous, electrifying, and unscripted, the stuff Lewis Carroll might have conjured up to ignite a child's imagination. I was on my way to New York to perform nightly in front of thousands of completely crazy towel-waving people.

The audience would play its own role in the action. Some would don bright-blue-and-neon-orange apparel, one would tie a Superman cape around his shoulders, and a college history professor would transform his persona into the Lone

Ranger of Shea Stadium. By the time I took the stage, they all would be screaming at my every action, every outcome marking me as a victor or a villain. Money would be at risk here, lots of money. I'd need to perform flawlessly under the bright lights and enormous pressure.

Players handle pressure in different ways—some block it, while others allow it to build. It is, in many careers, the sole determinant of success or failure. I look at pressure as a muscle, malleable, supple, and capable of being strengthened with exercise and resistance. I've learned over the years that I have to anticipate pressure and play through it, whatever form it takes. I can't hide from it; it will always find me. I need to own it before it owns me. I let the pressure build like a wave. I enjoy it cresting at certain times. I can ride it to take me places. I need to be realistic. The pressure is there, and it's always going to be there. I'm better listening to it, examining it, finding a way to coexist with it. I've played this scenario out in my mind hundreds of times.

As a boy, I fantasized batting against Warren Spahn and Sandy Koufax in the backyard of our little house in Norwood. I also pitched against Willie Mays and Hank Aaron, striking them out with men in scoring position. I was about to find out how close to reality those rehearsals were to the real pitcher's mound in Flushing Meadows.

For as long as I can remember I pictured myself playing baseball. I dreamed in baseball terms. I slept with my uniform on. I envisioned myself batting, hitting home runs, or pitching, striking out batters in the late innings. Looking back, there was no doubt. For reasons beyond my control, I practiced and pictured future events before they unfolded, first as a young boy in the backyard and later as an adolescent standing on a baseball field in between the lines. As I focused on the present moment, I trained myself to see myself in the future.

The commuter jet strained on its final approach into New York City. The roaring engines snapped me back to the present. Below, the big city was swallowing us even before we landed. The pilot came on the intercom to inform us that the local time was 1:00 pm and that we were coming in over Shea Stadium. The crowd was filling in and, from the tilt of the wings, I could see ten stanchions of candlepower. All the lights pointed at the pitcher's mound. The relics of the World's Fair stood reminiscent of the promise of the city, the big hopes, and the endless possibilities.

The landing jolted me. My steps had a beat of their own as I went down the passenger tunnel with a growing sense of urgency. I hurried to baggage claim, a stranger in a sea of commotion, grabbed the bags off the unyielding turnstile and hustled to the cab stand. A car broke eagerly in front of me, and I yelled, "Take me to Shea Stadium as fast as you can," a bit too theatrically. The next ten minutes did little to assuage my nerves, and soon we arrived at 123-01 Roosevelt Ave, Flushing Meadows, NYC. The cab skidded to a stop. "Hey buddy, we're here," the cabbie said. "It's a doubleheader today. Enjoy the games."

The Shea Stadium Players' Entrance was through a small door in the side of a gaudy Parthenon. Showing a bit of age, it was decorated with twenty-foot murals that depicted current and departed star players—Willie and Tug. The players' entrance was hidden in plain sight, no more than an indenta-tion, nondescript, an afterthought drawn in probably after the building plans were approved. The words over it read, "Home Team – Show Credentials."

Before I had a chance to say anything, the gate guard in a dark-gray uniform rose from his folding chair and put down his horse racing sheet, knocking a transistor radio over in the process. He pushed the metal door as far open as it would go, blocking half of the entrance with his police belt and gun. He said, "We're glad you're finally here. The pen needs some help. Like right now," as he pointed to the transistor radio on its side next to him.

In a few steps, we traveled down white-and-black linoleum tiles trodden down with years of deliveries and foot traffic. He ushered me ten feet to double glass doors with dark drapes drawn tight. With the touch of a button, the latch released from deep inside the door. We walked into an impressive clubhouse. It looked like a midtown men's club, quite a step up from County Stadium's bare-bones locker facility. I gulped down a surprise exclamation. "Wow!" He said, "Yea, quite a place, huh?"

The dark-blue carpeting was infused with gold marbling in the tread, elegant and tasteful, designed more for a lavish home or yacht. I didn't expect such luxury in a locker room. A leather seating area in the middle was a twenty-foot U-shaped plush couch. The lockers were constructed of blonde wood with metal mesh separations, each locker sporting a matching blonde stool in front. The tall wooden partitions stood three feet wide, ten lined up on one side and twenty on the other in the shape of an L. Every locker had a white nameplate on the top—Grote, Harrelson, Seaver . . . all famous players, all strangers to me. The room was too cavernous to be welcoming. It was a trophy room, a man cave with multiple television monitors all tuned in to the Mets station. I heard showers running and sensed the musty smell of a summer cottage rental. I dropped my luggage and wrestled with the canvas duffel. It was then that I noticed that a few more of the letters in the word "Brewers" had failed to make the trip.

Herbie Norman ambled around the corner. He was a one-man greeting committee, short, unshaven, wearing a wife-beater shirt, with a towel for a shawl. The shirt warned, "Mind Your Own Business." Herbie Norman was "Clubby" to everyone in this building. He was the home clubhouse manager. He had been at it for a long time. His job consisted of making order out of chaos, keeping everything nice and neat, washing all the players' laundry, and preparing a lavish spread of food after every game. He was the Mayor of Shea Stadium, the janitor of Flushing Meadows, and the boss man for everything that transpired in the Mets locker room. I would soon discover that he was also a legendary bit-part actor and a premier prankster.

"You Lockwood?" he greeted me, completely passing over the usual first meeting pleasantries. "What the hell kept you? We've been waiting all day for you. You were supposed to be here by game time. We're playing a doubleheader, you know. Hey, you need to get dressed and get your ass down to the bully."

Nice to meet you too, I thought. Ten steps into the National League, and already there was a sense of urgency. I started to tell Herb about the crazy cab ride, but he looked disinterested. "Drop those bags," he said. "We'll take care of your stuff. Your locker is over here," he pointed to the corner of the room where the bats were stacked up in wooden holders. I dropped my bags in front of a nameless locker. "Just leave all that stuff there, and I'll get one of the kids to hang it all up," Herbie said.

In the background, I heard Ralph Kiner, Hall of Famer and New York Mets television color commentator, describing in unapologetic terms the first few innings. He cautioned that those games were important and the Mets need to get off to a good start. He emphasized the need to pitch well and put some runners on base for the top of the lineup: Harrelson, Kingman, and Kranepool.

After a disappointing season in 1974, the Mets had made some major changes. In December, the team traded Tug McGraw for Del Unser and John Stearns and then, in February, acquired Dave Kingman, a tall, lanky right-handed hitter of prodigiously long home runs. The hope was that these changes would add strength to the lineup. The real heart of the team, though, was their starting pitching, which included Tom Seaver, heading for a 22-9 record and his third Cy Young Award, Jerry Koosman, and Jon Matlack. All were having strong years.

Life existed on a different level in NYC, and half an hour into my arrival, I got caught up in the fast-forward pace. My thoughts ran ahead of my actions; my hands were drenched in sweat. I couldn't find the buttons on my shirt. Putting on the uniform is a ritual practiced and refined over the years. I always put my long johns on first. I pulled a well-worn pair out of the duffel, rolled in a ball and cut hastily along the bottoms just above the knee in uneven lengths in a game with the Yankees. The hideous hack job mirrored my current state of mind. My underwear, with its crossed-out numbers, frayed elastic. My fingers stumbled as I reached for the white cotton sanitaries. The first pair I picked up were anything but sanitary. Running on automatic pilot, I pushed my hand inside, turned it inside out, and emptied a spoonful of sand. My heart beat faster with every new piece of clothing. I taped the sanitaries and wool stirrups with a once-around of athletic tape to keep them up. I stared at the mirror twenty feet away. The getup, combined with the horn-rimmed glasses, made me look like Clark Kent. Grabbing the home white uniform shirt off the hanger, I started unbuttoning it but was hampered by unworn, unrelenting loops. Losing patience with the process, I opted to shimmy into it partially unbuttoned. The shirt felt like a straitjacket. Too long, it fell down to my socks. It would need to be tucked in, which would hide most of my new number, whatever that might be.

Next, I pulled the uniform pants off the hanger, rushing now in a private panic. I sat on the stool and pushed one leg all the way down to the bottom. Showing a decided lack of flexibility, I caught my left toe on the crotch as I pulled on the second leg. I took one hop and then another. It's a good thing nobody was around to see this little act. Hopping turned into falling. I braced myself on the table where the spread of food had been carefully set out for the players between the games. I lunged at it in an effort to stay upright. Success. I got both feet on the ground, but my hand landed in the middle of the potato salad. Herbie was bound to be angry, but at least I didn't rip the pants. Pants finally on and bloused, I checked the mirror again to even them out—an old obsession. Herbie appeared out of nowhere and asked, "What size dome you got . . . here's a seven and a half. Try it on, but remember it will shrink a little when you sweat and here, my young friend, you will sweat." My transformation into a New York Metropolitan was now complete.

I pawed into my old duffel and searched for my cleats. They came out reluctantly, looking a bit worn with clumps of dirt in the spikes. "Grab these shoes," Herbie yelled to one of the clubhouse kids, who ran over and snatched the shoes before I could put them on. "We can't let you go out there looking like that," Herbie winked. I waited anxiously, watching the young man work furiously, putting the first shine in over a month on an old pair of cleats.

Like a junior high Choose Your Own Adventure book, I was an unfinished story. I represented a player with unrealized potential, unmet hopes. A power hitter as a rookie, I found a parade of demons in the form of breaking balls in the minor leagues. A hard-throwing starting pitcher in the American League, I couldn't find the strike zone in the late innings or a Major League Baseball contract that paid the rent. As my rail-skinny boyish physique gave way to a late-twenties frame and girth, so too had my role as a starter given way to that of a closer.

But once again I was skipping on to the next page. I was back in the big leagues and very much on stage. My shoes returned gleaming. Dressed from head to toe in Mets regalia, Herbie scrutinized me and gave a nod. He said, "Let's get going." He handed me a Mets warmup jacket and said, "Put this on." The whole getup was right out of central casting. Changing roles again, Herbie Norman was suddenly all business. "Come on," he said, and together we walked through the clubhouse door marked "To the Field – Players Only."

"I'll take you out there. You'll probably get lost by yourself," Herbie advised.

Despite my initial misgivings, I liked this guy. He seemed friendly and helpful. We scrambled aboard a golf cart and the four tires squealed as it headed to the bullpen area. Still somewhat in a fog, I felt great to be running full speed ahead. Trying to relax for a minute, I began to tell Herbie a little bio, practicing the lines I planned to use when I met my new teammates—I've played in the American League for six years leading up to a trip to the minors. I told him that I really didn't know anyone in the National League. "That's a shame," Herbie answered. "But you'll get to know them better after today." Little did I know that I was playing right into his scheme.

Herbie and I traveled down the dim cement labyrinth deep underneath Shea Stadium's grandstands. We heard the cheers and moans from the crowd, rising and falling on every pitch. The catacomb of tunnels and passageways appeared from both sides of the cart leading to unknown places deeper beneath the dome. The smooth driving surface under the wheels made the golf cart tires squeal at every turn as we headed towards the bullpen area. When we arrived in the bullpen, most of the players were seated. Two standing in the rear of the bullpen were talking animatedly with their hands.

Herbie braked to a stop and everyone turned to see the commotion. Talk about a grand entrance. "There you go," Herbie said, patting me on the shoulder, with a cat-in-the-hat grin on his face. I jumped out and headed over to the bullpen bench.

I started making my introductions. Most had their hats off, blue warmup jackets on. Some were standing in the back, others hung on the fence closer to the field. I started down the line shaking hands. "Hi . . . I'm Skip . . . Yes, Skip . . . Glad to meet you . . . Skip . . . Yea, Just got off the plane . . . Yep, it's my first time in the National League . . . I really don't know anyone in the League . . . Just got in from Tucson in the Pacific Coast League . . . Boy, what a long flight today . . . I'm a little tired . . . But I'm glad to be here . . . . How's the team doing?" Everything seemed to be going rather smoothly. I had almost said hello to everyone I could see, offering them all pleasantries you would normally say when you're introducing yourself to a new crowd.

I got down to the other end of the bench and started to take a seat, when the Expos bullpen coach yelled, "Hey rook . . . Are you shitting me? . . . How fucking stupid are you? . . . You're in the wrong bullpen, Dude. You play for the *other* team . . . the Mets . . . Look at your fucking uniform . . . This here is the Expos Bullpen. Your team's name is spelled entirely differently than this here." He pointed to the name on his jersey. Then he said, "Whatever you do, don't sit down in this here bullpen." I stood back up—Oh shit!

I looked over at Herbie, who was nearly hysterical. The other Expos were hugging each other, doubled over in laughter, unable to contain themselves. I had been pranked . . . and it was a good one.

This particular one act play, I would learn later, was Herbie's signature move and, in my case, perfectly choreographed and delivered with virtuosity. Welcome to New York. I wished I were on a harbor cruise with that elderly couple from the plane. I should not have been so self-absorbed that I didn't notice the insignia on their caps. But I didn't, and the humiliation from this lack of concentration would stay with me for a while. I wanted to hurl.

Back in the cart, the blood on my face was roughly the color of the piping on my METS jacket. "Sorry, Kid," Herbie gushed as I got back into the cart. "I couldn't resist. Thanks for being so good-natured." We were on the move again, this time a little more rapidly and deliberately. Herbie rerouted the golf cart back into the tunnel on to the right field bullpen and what I sincerely hoped was the home team's bullpen. Knowing clubhouse politics, I suspected this faux pas would be around for a while and probably grab more lasting headlines than my pitching ever would.

If it weren't for the pure absurdity of the situation and the ridiculous jubilation I expressed greeting my new teammates, I might have been able to laugh at myself. It was certainly not the first or the last time I would fall for a clubhouse prank, but at that present moment, I found it hard to breathe.

Herbie was still choking back little pig snorts of glee as we headed to the Mets bullpen. I couldn't wait to see what kind of a welcome I would receive there. Joe Pignatano, the bullpen coach, was wearing a significantly brighter blue jacket and a hat with more recognizable letters on it. Joe was on a matador-red bullpen phone talking to Rube Walker, the Mets pitching coach. Rube was standing four hundred feet away in the dugout, with his arms spread out wide and squinting and scowling toward right field where the Mets bullpen was located. He was asking, "Where is he?"

"Yea," Pignatano yelled into the phone. "Yep, he just got here. Sure. Next inning?"

The game was progressing poorly from the Mets' standpoint. Jerry Koosman, the starting pitcher, was pitching up in the strike zone. The Expos were feasting on poor pitch location. Ball one turned into a double in the gap. A curveball in the dirt advanced the runner to third and a ringing single scored him. A high throw from center allowed the runner on first to move up to second. The Mets needed a change.

Joe Pignatano—Piggy to his teammates—was a former catcher in his late forties. He played in the 1959 World Series with the LA Dodgers. A native New Yorker, he had a solid career but riddled with injuries. Joe stood stodgily square-shouldered and waved at me as the bullpen cart screeched to a stop. Herbie paused for a moment as I hopped out. I did not take comfort in the fact that he was waiting. Pignatano reached out his hand to shake mine. Already this seemed more reassuring, and he didn't look at all like a prankster. The frown on his face indicated a sense of urgency.

"You Lockwood?" he said.

This time I chose a more cautious route. "Let's start with who you are. Are you the Mets bullpen coach?" I asked him. He stared at me very strangely, and a moment of silence went by between us.

Realizing the ridiculousness of the question, he answered in a formal tone of voice, "Why yes . . . yes, I am." He continued to hold out his hand. Herbie remained in the golf cart snorting and giggling, which clearly increased my uncertainty. Staying overly formal, he said "And may I be the first one to welcome you to New York. I hope your stay is enjoyable." We held the handshake for an uncomfortable length of time. "Oh . . . that's right. They want you to warm up," he said to me. "You're going in as soon as you're ready."

This whole situation was a bit surreal. To be honest, I was still a little skeptical, half expecting another gotcha from Herbie or maybe Piggy, but if he really was the bullpen coach and if I really was going to pitch, I figured I'd better get my act together fast. I stepped into the clear light of the bullpen mound. It seemed that I was reenacting one of the dreams I had on the plane. I was feeling very small. I was entering a game to pitch in a stadium I couldn't have found with a tour map, for a team full of players I couldn't name without a roster, in a uniform that I had proven I could not identify. I needed to focus. It was going to take all my concentration to shake off the bumpy plane flight, the Indy cab ride to the stadium, and the sting of indignation at the hands of the Mets Clubbie—not to mention first-game jitters.

Moving quickly, spinning my arms around like a windmill, I began to stretch and jog toward the pitcher's mound at the far end of the warmup area. The lights from the forty-foot scoreboard blared down at me.

Ron Hodges, the bullpen catcher and my new teammate, slipped on his mitt and ran to the end of the bullpen. I stepped up on the mound and started throwing, not hard, more just playing catch. After about my fourth and fifth tosses, things on the field got a little more serious. "Hey," Joe yelled over the crowd noise. "You better pick up the pace a bit. Koosman is sucking wind out there."

Taking his words to heart, I stepped back on the mound a little to collect my thoughts. "Watch out," Pignatano shouted at me, pointing down at the back side of the slope. "Those red things are the league's best tomatoes." He sounded angry, and he also was pointing to some other kind of vegetable laying down there too. I looked down and saw that I just missed stepping on a large and very attractive tomato as well as an even larger zucchini; both looked like they had just been picked. Joe rushed over to move the vegetables to safety.

The third inning was not going well for the Mets. It looked like I might be making an earlier entrance than anticipated. I threw more purposefully now, starting to superimpose an imaginary hitter in the batter's box, a technique I'd used throughout my career. Unfortunately, I couldn't envision who that hitter on the Expos might be, since I only vaguely knew a couple of pitchers and a coach, who were all still in the Expos bullpen.

Koosman was getting kicked around. The first batter, Tim Foli, tripled over the center fielder's head. Gary Carter flew out to right scoring the run, making the score 3-0. The next batter, José Morales, singled to right. Bob Bailey swung at the first pitch and hit a moon shot over the wall in left, scoring two. The score was 5-0 now. After two pitches in the dirt, Larry Parrish spanked the third pitch up the middle for a single. With a man on first, Pete Mackanin hit a towering shot to right, which missed going out by only a few feet. Piggy, standing next to me, waved his hat to Rube Walker, the pitching coach, who was standing on the dugout steps looking directly at us. "You are ready, right?" he said to me after already signaling to Rube. "It looks like you're in." It was too late to correct or amend that piece of miscommunication. I shrugged in resignation. I was going in. Looking down, my feet were taking me towards the open bullpen door and thousands of blood-thirsty, partially inebriated fans. My moment had arrived. I was fresh meat.

The bullpen catcher slapped me five and gestured toward an open door. The Mets bullpen cart was waiting on the right field grass. I was on my way. Things were catapulting from the absurd to the outrageous.

The conveyance for the trip into the unknown was shielded by a giant Mets hat with a saucer-shaped fur-covered brim for a nose. We were pimped out. The cart-hat and I traversed a

quizzically than before, openly wondering if I could pitch or even if I could see. I certainly didn't look like anything he would have drawn up. His eyes wandered to my glasses, and he looked away. There was a shrug of resignation in his reaction. His body language was saying, "You need to prove something right here, right now." He knew that the space I occupied on the mound was vital to the team. We stood together for a second or two.

"Barry Foote?" I asked, realizing how stupid it sounded as soon as I said it. "Yea," Stearns said half laughing. "You heard of him . . . Are you okay, dude?" I nodded affirmatively.

"So," he continued. "What are we featuring today?" I was having trouble breathing. I gulped a long pull of air surrounding Flushing Meadows. Sounding like a man on a ventilator, I held everything in for another few seconds. John was just standing there bobbing from one foot to another. Finally, I was able to get out, "I'm mainly a fastball pitcher, not much else." I continued, "I throw a cross-seamer . . . Sometimes it has some life to it, and I can spin a breaking ball, but it's mainly for show."

He didn't respond, looking more vacant than before. He seemed far away and wrapped in his own personal thoughts. He returned to me. "Shit, you're going to need some kind of heater today," he said. "This guy's a fastball hitter with men on base. Listen, let's get ahead of him, and if he doesn't kill you or hit it out, I'll come out again before the next hitter comes up." He left and strutted towards home, shaking his head.

****

INSIGHT PITCH

My back muscles tighten. A new ache arches across my shoulders. Back behind the plate John flips his mask back down into go mode. I sense he likes the gladiator feel of the mask and the catcher's gear.

The danger here is to switch on autopilot. I cannot slip into anything automatic. I need a focal point. I need to turn off the crowd noise surrounding me. I have to get oxygen to my muscles, relax my grip pressure on the ball, and, within the confines of the seven warmup pitches, find a release point out in front of me that will take the ball on a downward arch and into the strike zone. One trick I've used in the past was to picture a fence about five feet high right in front of me; that image makes me get my arm up high enough to make sure the ball is on a downward path. In thinking about that fence, the warmup tosses grow more comfortable, one adding to the next. My feet feel sticky in the unyielding heavy clay on the mound. I decide not to fight it and adjust to the solid surface. I throw the first couple of warmup pitches. John catches them in the strike zone.

I hear Yogi on the bench chirping, "Come on Chip, throw strikes." I want to throw strikes, but I am still having problems with the glasses. To stall for time, I bend over and pick up the rosin bag, which I don't need and rarely use. The rosin bag makes me lose focus for a second, and I come within a whisker of dropping the ball again. I save it at the last minute with a fast swipe of my free hand. The rosin bag drops on my foot, spreading white dust all over the right half of the rubber. I kick it in disgust, and it disappears over the edge of the mound. Stearns looks out at me shaking his mask. The crowd, impatient with the delay in the action, chants "bush league."

My third warmup pitch lands in the dirt. The fourth is so wide it nearly hits the bat boy, who has come out to give the umpire more balls. Stearns lobs the last ball back to me in the shape of a question mark. I look down and take a deep breath . . . I need to focus . . . to execute a pitch sequence that I have practiced a million times. I need to hinge my wrist. I need to release the ball, spinning the seams like I am pinching a bug. I stare down at my harlequin cleats; one white shoe dusted with rosin, one black shoe shined with impunity by the clubhouse boy. Time to stop clowning around. Time to step up.

Finally, I am ready. I guess. The first pitch flies unsuccessful. It's a ball inside, barely catchable, but missing Foote, who is, as advertised, diving towards the plate. On the second pitch, he guesses right and hits a rope single to left field, scoring Parrish from third. Mackanin stops at second. Stearns, true to his word, joins me on the mound. "Don't worry about that. Concentrate on the next batter, Carrithers. He's the pitcher. You can pitch him up in the strike zone. We'll start him out away and then get him out with a heater inside. Got it?" Yogi continues to yell, "Come on Chip. Throw strikes."

Don Carrithers takes the first pitch for a strike on the outside corner. The second pitch catches the outside corner too. The third pitch has a little hair on it. It eats him up as it travels a rising trajectory, wrapping him up inside. Runners are still at first and second and the score is six to zero.

Pepe Mangual, a free-swinging infielder—called the "Speedy Puerto Rican" by his teammates—has the ability to hit the ball anywhere. The first pitch to him is a strike, a little bit higher than I want, right down the middle, not an optimal location. Pepe takes it, probably taken by surprise. He looks out as if to say, "How in the world can you throw me that pitch in this situation . . . Don't you know who I am?" Kicking some loose dirt toward the rosin bag on the grass, I stare back at him. The second pitch is just ugly. My glasses fog again, and the mound isn't comfortable because of the enormous dirt crater-wall five feet in front of me. I hang on to the ball entirely too long. It travels, with a fair amount of velocity, behind Pepe on a line dangerously close to the bat boy kneeling near the on-deck circle. It careens off the pads behind home plate, narrowly missing the stands.

On the positive side, the pitch is hard and carries a message. Mangual jackknifes. It misses him. Stearns tries to make a circus stab. The runner moves up. Stearns steps out in front of the plate and under-hands it back. "Did you mean to do that . . . Come on . . . Get your shit together . . . Throw strikes." I step back on the mound and take another deep breath. Looking in at Stearns for the sign, I notice he's taking a slightly wider football lineman stance. John puts down two fingers, indicating he wants a curve. I call timeout. The fans boo.

Stearns comes out to the mound. "I don't have a number two," I say using the numeric name of the curveball.

"I thought you said that you have a spinner," he says.

"I do, but I don't throw it very much." I shake my head sheepishly.

"Okay," he says sarcastically. "From now on when I put down two fingers . . . just for you . . . it doesn't mean curve; it means a twice-as-fast fastball." He laughs out loud and heads back to the plate to test this new strategy. I go back to the mound ensconced as a one-pitch pitcher having a strong feeling of simpatico with my catcher. Mangual takes strike two on the outside corner, not

believing it's coming from the same pitcher who threw the first pitch. The third strike is the best pitch of the inning. It has late movement, whizzes past, biting the inner two inches of the strike zone. Pepe swings half-halfheartedly. He is out, and he knows it.

I turn and retreat towards the Mets dugout, releasing a deep breath. The inside of my new jersey feels clammy. My jaw and neck loosen a little as I head for the safety of the dugout. Nausea nips at the pit of my stomach. The glasses are completely useless. I head in the direction of the first base foul line, which I hop over. My emotions are running on high like an engine stuck in first gear. I find a spot on the bench and collapse into the padding.

****

In collapsing on the bench, I am suddenly snapped back into reality. I take my hat off, placing my glasses inside it. I notice the cardboard packing material still in the hat. I start to remove it when Rube Walker, Mets pitching coach, comes over and sits down to introduce himself, an act of civility that is greatly appreciated. I move quickly to pick up the glasses before he sits on them. Rube speaks in a slow southern drawl.

"Are you doing alright?" he asks and hands me a towel. "When was the last time you pitched?" I tell him, "Yesterday, in Tidewater." "They made you pitch when you were in Tidewater?" he said incredulously. "You were just supposed to hang out for a game or two, until we cleared up our roster." I shrug. "They asked me if I wanted to pitch an inning, and I didn't know if I was coming up here today or tomorrow, so I said I would."

"Okay. Okay. You made some good pitches that inning. Stearns says you have good velocity. We're going to send you out again for the fourth. You okay?" "I'm fine," I replied. "You have a string of right-handers coming up—Foli, Carter, and Dwyer. Keep the ball down and keep on throwing strikes," he cautioned.

The Mets made three quick outs on only a handful of pitches and, before the rooster crowed three times, I was heading back to the mound. The glasses were getting better but were not completely clear. I ran back to the middle of the field and, to my delight, eight players whose names I didn't know ran with me to take up their positions. Other players hung on the rail, and some spit tobacco at paper cups on the dirt track in front of them. They offered encouragements like, "Get ahead of this guy, come on kid, throw strikes, bear down and get the first batter out. Vamos."

****

I feel a tap of someone's glove to my backside, a get-a-grip gesture.

The trip takes me across the first base foul line. I hop over it like it's a snake.

The pitching mound is pretty beaten-up. It did not receive the same grooming the infield got in between innings. The rubber is partially hidden.

I'm trying to keep my emotions hidden too. My thoughts are running smoother and more predictably. The hair on my arms stands at full attention. I exhale deeply, but it turns into a cough, which turns into a choke. My focus during the warmup pitches is to find the right grip pressure to direct the ball to a specific location . . . and not to puke.

Even though Stearns knows what the pitch selection is going to be, protocol compels him to go through the motions of giving the signs. The problem is, I can't see his fingers because the moisture inside the lens is restricting my visual acuity. So, having faced this problem before, I make an adjustment . . . to my stance. I know from experience that the only way to see the signs is to use my peripheral vision and look through the edges of the lens, not through the middle. I make a quarter-body rotation towards first base. It gives the impression to the batter, the umpire, and the fans that I am not looking at the catcher. It also is making the bat boy extremely nervous.

Stearns runs to the mound, "Man, what are you doing? You really can't see the signs? Can you see the batter?" "I'm okay. The glasses usually clear up on their own. It just takes a few seconds. Really, I'm okay. Let's go, before Yogi gets nervous. I can finish this out," I say. Another call, "Come on Chip. What the fuck?" arrives at the mound, with Yogi's voice connected to it.

Foli, the first batter, gingerly steps into the batter's box adjusting his own aviator glasses. He taps the plate and stares out at me. His face contorts with a mixture of determination and concern. My guess is he's going to swing early, probably at the first pitch he can get a bat on. No sense in facing some crazy rookie up from the boonies, who throws hard and apparently can't see. Just as I suspect, he goes after the first two pitches, fouling them off close to the plate. I put a little spinner in the dirt for show, and the next pitch surprises Tim. It's a little high in the strike zone and rides off the plate. He swings, but has no chance of hitting it. The ump calls, "Stree-rike."

Gary Carter flies out to right, and I walk Dwyer and Jorgensen on eight pitches, none of which are very close to the plate. The bat boy moves closer to the dugout, and Stearns assumes a defensive lineman stance again. Larry Parrish comes up as an unwilling participant in this melodrama. He hits a weak dribbler to Phillips at short, who scoops it up, one step on the infield grass, and throws across his body to Milan at second, timing the play perfectly to force the runner. Five outs under my belt.

Rube Walker meets me at the dugout steps, usually a sign that I am being taken out. He escorts me to the bench, sits down next to me, and says, "This is the first game of a doubleheader and our pen has been worked like a mule at haying time. Yogi wants to get another inning out of you. You up for it?" He knows the answer before he asks. I agree, but it's really too late anyway, as the Mets have already made two outs.

The fifth inning starts quickly. I feel a little more relaxed; the urge to puke has subsided. My glasses are still fogged on the left side, but at least I can look directly at the catcher and get the signs, which are predictably going to be a number one followed by another number one.

On the second pitch, Mackanin grounds to Wayne Garrett at third base, who takes the ball on a short hop and darts a textbook throw to first. I am starting to think I really like the National League when Barry Foote guesses fastball first pitch and gets all of it. He hits a towering fly to left. As Bob Murphy, Mets announcer would say, "That's way outta here." It's not really all that far, but it ends up being caught by one of my new friends in the Expos pen. He raises it up nice and high so I can see it. I pout around the fringes of the mound while he trots the bases.

Carrithers, the opposing number, hits a grounder to short and Pepe Mangual flies out to center, the ball making a thud in the middle of Del Unser's glove. He points the little prize at me as he runs in. On the bench Rube gives me a high five and every member of the team comes over to me and says, "Nice job." Yogi says, "Good going, Chip. Go get ready for the second game."

****

My first day on the mound at Shea was historic—at least personally. After the games, I tried to luxuriate on my stool, but celebrating is a no-no after losing both games of a doubleheader. I did enjoy a few muffled laughs about my wild pitches with my locker neighbor, Bob Myrick. The bat boy kept his distance, and Herbie offered a conspiratorial wink. I was in desperate need of a good night's sleep. The Mets Traveling Secretary, Lou Niss, came over to my locker and told me that he had booked overnight reservations at the Travelers Inn near La Guardia, just a short cab ride from the stadium.

When I arrived, I was surprised at how busy the lobby was so late in the evening. The bar was packed, and every inch of the circular ottoman in the lobby was filled with flimsy attired hot mommas. Much to my surprise, the desk clerk recognized my name and warmly welcomed me to New York. He inquired as to how long I would need the room. I guess I should have been forewarned by his raised eyebrows when I said I would probably stay for a couple of days.

CHAPTER 5

LONGBALL: POLO GROUNDS, 1962

"All the power on earth can't change destiny."
(*The Godfather Part III*)

THE TRIP FROM Norwood, Massachusetts, to New York City should take about five hours, but on this sultry summer day the roads were crowded, and traffic crawled along at a snail's pace, significantly lengthening our journey. I rode shotgun, that coveted spot relinquished in a moment of sisterly acquiescence, partially in recognition of the importance of the day but mostly so my sister Betty could build an Afghan-inspired canopy dollhouse in the rear seat. My well-worn baseball glove rested comfortably on my lap while my stiffly starched jeans stuck to the seat. A sports talk show spewed out over the radio. The Red Sox had lost the night before, and the announcers were an hour into their negative rant.

Dad's driving was ponderously slow and erratic. Unfamiliar with the roads, Dad pulled over again and again to check the map, not trusting my mother's nonexistent navigational skills as the car inched near the soaring towers of the light stanchions of the Polo Grounds. Late in the afternoon we finally found our team-recommended motel destination and settled in for my date with destiny.

When I awoke the next morning, my stomach ached. I was heading into new territory, where I would be on display. I'd never been selected to a national team before. I breathed in with mountainous delight and breathed out with an equal measure of dread. My nervous fingers tapped a Beatles tune on the vinyl window sill. My unfocused gaze relayed the anxiousness at getting my first crack on a big stage, on a field that looked, to my wide open eyes, the size of Texas.

Just making the team was an honor. Walking into the stadium was the thrill of a lifetime. At the age of sixteen, I was inside an actual big-league clubhouse for the first time. An air of history hung heavy in the hallowed place where Mays and Aaron sat. Mesmerized, I took it all in. I marveled at the polish on the lacquered wooden lockers. A bat rack, bats fitting barrel-down with the players' numbers on the handles, beckoned countless stories of past glory days.

Players were introducing themselves and figuring out how to get into their assigned gray visitor's uniform. A tower of a man ambled over, dressed in the same fancy uniform I was struggling to assemble. "Hi, my name is Haywood Sullivan."

I reached up and shook hands. My fingers felt like they were delving into a popcorn box . . . all bumps and angles. Ex-Major League catcher Haywood Cooper Sullivan was the coach of the Hearst All-Star Team. He was a huge man, with a gentle smile and quiet wisdom behind his glasses, who would become a manager, general manager, and club owner of the Red Sox. Our paths were destined to cross many times over the next twenty years. "I've been looking forward to meeting you. Congratulations on a great high school career. I'm one of the coaches today. There's some great talent in this room. Hope you can relax and enjoy the day.

"We're going to take batting practice and infield. Later we will announce the starting lineup and the reserve players on the team. Right now, the starting third baseman is Jerry McMahon from Chicago, but I understand he might not be feeling good and might be scratched. I want you to practice as if you're going to start and, if you don't, I promise to get you into the game and get you an at-bat. Okay?" he said.

He didn't wait for me to answer. "Great to meet you, get dressed, we're going to take pictures in half an hour out near the dugout. Are your mom and dad here to see you play?" he inquired. He seemed pleased to hear that they were. "Hope to get a chance to meet them some time."

In the summer of 1962, the Polo Grounds in New York was host to an exhibition game between the US All-Star Team and the NY All-Star Team. It was a one-day contest that would showcase the best high school baseball players from the East Coast to the West Coast. Eighteen hundred boys tried out for the team. In the Hearst Sandlot finals, high school "phenoms" from all over the country competed. I made the cut.

The Polo Grounds was an imposing place, both in size and history. Burned to the ground in 1911, it was replaced by a structure reminiscent of the Roman Coliseum. The roof had eight decorative panels, freeze-frame allegories to gladiators, one for each National League team. *Baseball Magazine* at the time called it "the mightiest temple ever erected . . . to the Goddess of Sports." The field was shaped like an elongated horseshoe. Right field was a mere two hundred eight feet away from the plate and the pole in left only twenty-two feet farther, but center field was a monstrous five hundred five feet out and the hitting alleys measured four hundred fifty feet. "To the batter standing at home plate," Jon Eig, reporter with the *Herald Tribune* wrote, "center could have been in the Hamptons."

I was not supposed to start. I was only a sophomore in high school and, more importantly, had no advanced press. However, the favored starter from Chicago suffered a broken finger in a game three days before and was brokenheartedly relegated to the bench.

Baseball history is made in the space between home plate and the pitcher's mound, an area measured exactly sixty feet six inches. On this day, the lights would shine on everyone equally, but only a few would reflect that radiance back. On this day the connection between a seasoned wooden bat and a fastball, a mediocre one at that, would make tomorrow's news and ensure my spot in baseball lore.

I stepped in to face the tall lefty from Brooklyn, New York, the starter for the NY All-Stars. His picture had adorned the back cover of both New York morning sports pages, a handsome young face, grinning, with the words "can't miss" in caps below. The press had predicted that his signing and uniform

ceremonies were only a day or two away, the destination dependent on this game's outcome, but it was assumed that he would
most likely choose to wear Yankee pinstripes. I never got his
name. He would likely remember mine for a long time. The
next day his name would appear only parenthetically in the cap-
tion below the photo on page one of the *New York Times* sports
page. Its headline would read, "Boston lad makes a big swing."

****

*The first pitch is a big overhand curve shaped like a barrel. It's
slow and travels low into the dirt. The umpire calls "ball one." I
know what's coming next. It has to be a fastball, juicy enough for
hitting, probably right down the middle because the Phenom—
whatever his name is—doesn't want to get behind in the count.
I see it early. It's spinning tightly but not quite as fast as I would
have imagined. I am right, and I am ready.*

*Things slow down just before the lefty releases the pitch. I can
see his lead leg arch, bend, and step into the landing spot as he
grunts a little to give something extra. On route, I can see the ball's
four seams spinning . . . a fastball, just like I thought. I can see the
red sewn stitching tumbling. My muscles want it, and they start to
flex as it approaches. My quick response muscles fire in.*

*My left foot finds the hard dirt in front of the batter's box,
digs in, and torques inside the cleats. I start the swing to time the
contact. "Be patient and let it get here . . . then be quick," I say
to myself. Reflexes take over in the 0.2 seconds. I turn on it as it
starts for the inside corner. I don't want to go too quickly and pull
it foul, but I do want to get it out in front of the plate.*

Looking so big, so round, and so inviting I have to exhibit enormous patience. The Louisville Slugger I'm holding is thirty-six inches long and weighs thirty-three ounces. The heaviness of the ash wood is well-balanced and, from the first time I picked it up, measuring it with simulated swings, I knew I had found a trustworthy partner.

I've taken this swing thousands of times, first with a backyard full of rocks of all sizes and colors and a broken broomstick handle. I'd throw up one rock at a time, hitting one . . . then another . . . then another. For hours every day, hands bleeding. No reason more than the urgency of destiny.

It's like the bat is swinging itself. The thin end moves first, driving down and out and the thick part beginning to gain momentum. The fingers compressed, working together, with knuckles lined up just a notch above the knob, release through the hitting zone free and easy.

I don't feel the ball connect with the K55 model, which is always a good thing—it means that the ball has made contact within the sweet spot near the Louisville label, where the grain gets tight. The ball, ricocheting off the bat, sounds like a bullet. A sharp snap echoes against the Polo Grounds left field stands, empty except for a few pigeons who take flight. The fence is three hundred eighty-four feet to the power alley. The blast boomerangs back as I finish the swing and toss the bat towards the home dugout. The ball, on the other hand, sails outbound, heading out over the shortstop, who's standing still and looking up helplessly. It continues to carry, heading toward left center.

I complete the swing and sense the roar of the crowd. The left fielder takes a couple of strides backwards, but he needs a ticket for this one. It hits ten rows up and makes a hollow clank against the metal frame of the empty bleacher seats. I've never played in front of such a big crowd and feel the compression of air as they collectively react.

I head for first down the same path Willie Mays has taken, with the same feeling, "I got that one on the screws." On route to first base, a picture of Willie, running sort of tilted, leggy and swinging his arms, flashes in my mind. I mimic the cock of the head and the exaggerated strides. The first base coach for the US team, Clyde King, sees my unusual stride dancing toward him in the first base coaching box and says, "Nice hit kid, make sure you step in the middle of every bag"—good instructions for an overly excited sixteen-year-old heading toward second base and racing towards his future.

****

The Polo Grounds were jammed that day with family and friends along with a coterie of baseball scouts. Scouts play a vital role in baseball. They hunt down and evaluate talented players all over the country. It is not any easy task. This event was a prime shopping spree, a showcase of talent. You could see the ash tips of cigars from the dugout as they craned to see what just happened. You could hear the program pages turning in unison as they all tried to find out who just hit the cover off the ball. And they did. They located my name, my school, my high school coach's name, my parents' names, and probably my favorite ice cream.

Professional teams relied on the services of career scouts as well as part-timers called bird dogs. These men were tobacco-chewing hangers-on. Some had been fringe players, others simply liked going to games with a stopwatch around their necks. They followed high school and college teams like a pack of mad dogs, hoping to sniff out some warm meat they called talent. Most could justify their Lincoln Town Cars and their well-padded expense accounts. Scouts talked among themselves about individual talent but reserved their inner instincts for their board rooms. Despite the outward camaraderie inherent in their profession, an element of cut-throat competition reigned supreme.

In a few years, the league would create a central scouting bureau to save money and time. For the most part, the scouting bureau has been successful. It has given more amateur players a chance to get into the system or at least get a chance to audition. In the mid-1960s, eyeballs ruled, and the rating system on young talent sounded more like a rating chart for purchasing a car. The scouts talked about wheels and hoses as if the players were auto parts. The scouts came equipped with clipboards and stopwatches. They talked to individual players and were especially interested in what the coaches had to say.

The scouts showed up early before the games, spoke with some of the parents in the stands, and stayed longer to introduce themselves to a player or two. They were scouting for talent, scoring the skills in five discrete areas: hitting power, hitting for average, arm strength, running speed, and that intangible something called heart. The home run I hit out of the Polo Grounds put me out on the lot. I was a new name on the list for the scouts to check out. Facts were facts. I could hit with power. I could hit for average. I had real good foot speed and an exceptional arm. I had each category covered in spades. There were lots of intangibles, though, and no one could accurately predict the future.

CHAPTER 6
MONEYBALL, 1964

THE BLACK LIMOUSINE barreled down the pothole-ridden road, breaking here and there, kicking up dust, looking for the numbers on the cookie-cutter houses. It skidded to a stop, over-shooting #222, the weather-beaten green-sided ranch, by a few yards. Like a scene from a movie, the driver, mustachioed and decked out in a blue suit and cap, stepped out first and marched around the polished front grill to open the rear passenger side door. Cigar smoke was first to exit the stately vehicle, leaking past the leather interior and wafting into the late June sky.

Over the past few years my high school baseball accolades, trophies, and newspaper coverage continued in what seemed to be a never-ending upward spiral. Today all of that was history, and I was ready to turn the page onto a new and unpredictable professional career. How exactly all that was going to happen was not clear. Coming on the heels of earning fourteen high school varsity letters and a starting position on the US All-Star Team, as well as two MVP nominations, the New

England high school fifty-yard dash record outdoors (which would hold up for thirty years), and achieving the highest academic honors in an all-boys Catholic high school, I was riding high (although I was having trouble adjusting to my new contact lenses, but that's a whole different story).

My father was telling everyone who would listen that I was going to sign a Major League Baseball contract today. My dad, Claude Sr., was usually a man of few words, 5-foot-5 at the top of his head where all the hairs stood at attention. During the past few months, even my unassuming father had gotten caught up in a media frenzy. The events of the next few hours would determine if it all was merely hype.

The summer of 1964 was the year before the professional baseball "draft" would kick in, limiting prospects to only one bidding team. It was the last time Major League Baseball scouts had unfettered access to amateur players. Team-specific scouts brought high-sounding promises and low-budget checkbooks to untested talents in living rooms across the country in the hope of nabbing a green-behind-the-ears youngster to sign a piece of parchment. The scouts' reputations were also on the line. By signing a prospect who made a contribution to the big league team, a scout's intuition (and expense account) was validated.

The day arrived with all the markings of a scorcher, but the real rise in temperature would come later during a conversation between a seventeen-year-old prospect and a Vice President of Baseball Operations for the Kansas City Athletics around a four by six Formica table.

Like most other seventeen-year-olds, I started the day off in front of the mirror, except my mirror was not related to vanity; that would come later. My mirror was housed in the basement. It stood a full six feet tall and cantilevered slightly against a cinder block wall, offering a full torso view. Observing my reflection in this mirror had become an obsession. The mirror was a mental conditioning tool. This was my batting mirror, and I stood in front of it for hours every day.

The mirror was there to reflect every swing of the bat . . . hour after hour, swing after swing. I had the heaviest major league bat the sporting goods store had to sell, a thirty-six ounce K55, the kind reportedly used by Hank Aaron. I would later find out in person that Hank used to swing a much lighter bat. By the age of seventeen, I had thousands of swings imbedded in my head. The muscle motion had become fluid and comfortable, even with the heaviest bat.

My morning mirror ritual was set in place in Little League. Over the years I discovered that a level swing, with no "hitch" or premature hand motion, was the secret to hitting all kinds of pitches—curves, heaters, and changeups. I hit toward a makeshift net so as not to break any more windows. Working through my routine, I'd memorize how it felt to swing and visualize how I looked swinging. I was imprinting. I was projecting.

Swinging sounds emanated from the basement again and again on this pivotal morning. I slid on my winter gloves and began swinging faster and faster, one after another, without let-up. I took a batter's stance and pictured a pitch being thrown and pictured myself hitting the ball with a complete swing and follow through. Inside balls, outside balls, I'd continue visualizing doubles to right and liners off Fenway's Green Monster. Each swing had a meaning, and each swing had a purpose. Every action was a rehearsal. Every gesture had an underlying objective.

Throwing came next. Throwing from a standing position was a problem, as the drop ceiling from the close floor jounces under the kitchen above was too low. Adjustments had been made years ago. I would throw half of the throws sidearm . . . mostly running forward as if fielding a weakly hit ball crossing on to the infield grass and making a quick snap throw to first. The other balls I would pitch from a made-up mound. Today's mound consisted of a shoebox cover duct-taped to the floor. Windups worked off the improvised mound.

"When you have men on base," my father would say, "you have to be quick to the plate, but you don't want to give up any velocity."

I imagined faking the runner back to the base or catching him not paying attention and slipping in a quick pitch. Most of all I enjoyed just holding the ball and "seeing" the batter's muscles tense and tighten before I threw the inside smoke that he would not be able to get around on. With glove in hand, I'd mimic the actions of snatching the catcher's throw back to me. Then I'd work on the bender. I mirrored two kinds of breaking pitches—one that broke two to seven and one I called the hammer, which was more twelve to six, curving straight down more than across. I'd recreate a specific situation when making these pitches.

"Never let the batter see you smile, and never let anyone read your face while you're on the mound. Big league hitters live right here," my father would say and point to the middle of the zone. "Big league pitchers live here," he'd say, pointing to the black rubber circumference around the plate.

Today was going to be a day of old-school give-and-take, something in which I had absolutely no experience. It would also be a time for listening and reading the sincerity of gestures and facial expressions, a tough challenge for a starry-eyed young boy—and family. All the practice of level swings with no "hitch" would have to translate into level understanding.

The major questions of who, what, when, and where would be answered today. Decisions made on this day would determine whether I would join the ranks of the big leagues as a pitcher or a hitter, or maybe I would be better off going to college where I would get a little bigger and, hopefully, smarter.

Five teams indicated interest in talking to me—three wanted to sign me as an infielder, one wanted me to play outfield, and one wanted me as a pitcher. The Baltimore Orioles, the Boston Red Sox, the Houston Colts, the Kansas City Athletics, and the Detroit Tigers were scheduled to visit. Their scouts had followed me throughout my junior and senior years, coming to Catholic Memorial's home field and traveling to away games all over New England.

Having completed my morning mirror exercises, I sat down in the kitchen with my dad. "Today should be an interesting day," my father said, with a facial expression mimicking the

Cheshire cat in *Alice in Wonderland*. "Let's take one team at a time. Listen and see what they have to say."

The Boston Globe was tossed up on the front porch by a paperboy who had a pretty good arm of his own. Jumping immediately over to the *Globe*'s sports page, I found a sidebar story: "Local baseball All-Star poised to be offered a potentially record-breaking pro contract."

The article pointed out that rarely had a New England athlete been so highly sought after, having been scouted for two seasons and having had every move charted, analyzed, and scored up or down in the value chart. The writer asserted that being offered a "contract," and maybe a substantial one, was not only possible but probable. The *Globe* suggested that this competitive bidding contest could escalate as the day wore on. It went on to say that baseball was close to instituting a moratorium on big bonuses and that this might be the last year we would see such competition for young, untested talent.

I folded back the paper and put it aside. Conversation ceased completely. Dad and I stared at each other as we waited for the future to unfold.

"Hey Mom, I don't feel so good," my ten-year-old sister, Betty, moaned as she arrived at breakfast. Betty sniffled a little and scratched at a small red dot on her cheek. "What are these things on my face?" Elizabeth Barbara was a precocious middle-schooler. She was an alter ego, a "don't get ahead of yourself" influence over me. Never one to be overlooked, she smirked as if to say I'm going to have an impact on this day after all. She was running a temperature and a small cluster of red dots circled her left eye. "You've got the chicken pox, get back into bed," yelled my mother. I responded with a nervous laugh, "Well that makes things a little more interesting."

Betty took out some crayons and free-handed a picture of a little girl with spaghetti hair, a very sad face, and red spots all over the place. We taped it to the front door. She drew a few spots on the stairs too before she was sent back to her room for the duration—a dire warning to the new arrivals due in less than an hour.

At 9:35 am, the telephone rang on the wall of the kitchen. "It's for you," my father said and handed over the receiver. The ten-inch cord didn't permit much privacy. I stood with one arm on the fridge, which kicked on, creating a deafening sound. I said, "Hello," half holding my breath. The call was from the Houston Colt 45's, a National League team whose scout I had only spoken to in passing.

"Hello," I repeated, gulping for air. "Yep, this is he . . . Hi, I sure do. Thanks. Yes, it's going to be a big day. Thank you, I feel lucky to have played so well my senior year."

A few questions ensued.

"Oh yes, I passed all the classes and graduated last Saturday . . . Yes, I would like to sign. I believe that today will give me the choices I'm looking for."

And then, "Okay. No. No one has arrived here yet. You're the first team I've talked to."

I stayed calm through the next set of questions. "No, I haven't, and I won't make up my mind until I get a chance to talk to everyone."

"Okay. What do you have in mind?"

Wow, I thought to myself. *Thirty-five thousand dollars and you want me to play the outfield.* Over on the other side of the kitchen, the conversation brought a rather theatrical fist pump from my father, still perched at the kitchen table staring at his unfinished pancakes.

It was at that point that I wrapped up the conversation. "Well, this is quite a surprise. Say, I haven't talked to anyone else, and I promised a couple of teams that they would have a chance to talk before I made up my mind, but thank you. I will call you back soon." I hung up the phone. One-for-one. I was on my way!

The Boston Red Sox contingent arrived soon after, headed by Milt Bolling, two scouts, and a media representative from a Boston news station. Of course, I would love to play for the home team, but I would also love to be guaranteed a promising path to the big leagues. No such guarantee was forthcoming.

As the day wore on, my options became more intriguing. Substantial sums of money were being dangled before me. Several offers sat on the table. One organization wanted me to sign as an outfielder. They would assure me a spot in A ball this summer with the promise of a non-roster invite to spring training in February. Another could offer no guarantees but was confident I'd be able to work my way up the organization as a pitcher. One team representative stressed the importance of keeping my options open. He wanted me to report to the instructional league in a utility role and let the coaches there determine my position. While the money was enticing, their lack of commitment to my future was disconcerting.

For the price of a few cigars, my father had agreed to let the Kansas City Athletics go last. He thought that Kansas City would ultimately be the best team for me and make the best offer. Charlie Finley, the salt-tongued owner of the Kansas City Athletics, was intent on constructing a colorful, young team. Engaged in a coast-to-coast talent search, he was aggressively pursuing the best high school and college ballplayers available. That summer he would sign over thirty teenagers who would become the nucleus of the powerhouse teams in the 1970s and 1980s.

Charlie's right-hand man, an insurance executive and general manager by the name of Pat Friday, flew into Logan Airport and took a limo to Norwood to meet Bill Enos, the A's scout who had done all of the legwork. A burst of smoke emanated out of the limo as Mr. Friday swung his wing-tips out of the back seat, stood up, and buttoned his jacket, looking like a world-renowned dignitary or an ambassador from another country. He was followed by Enos, and the two swaggered toward the door that said "Danger: Chicken Pox."

They exuded confidence as they ducked their heads to enter the small house. The conversation began with a warm welcome, a little bow of deference to my mother Florence, and a discussion about chicken pox. Pat quickly got down to business and told me that they were counting on me to be their third baseman in the future. He assured me I would be on the fast track to the big leagues and an offer was made.

After thirty minutes of small talk, we came to a point where a certain question would be asked. Dad sensed that it was coming and got up from the table rather abruptly and looked at me directly and said, "Son, this is a decision you should make by yourself without my interference." He padded his way down the hall, scuffing the hardwood floor en route to his bedroom, where Mom sat praying the rosary.

Pat and I were sitting across from each other at the table. "Push that pen over here," I said to Pat, gesturing in its direction. Pat smiled, fatherly, and nodded his agreement with this decision. "My pleasure, young man, and welcome to the Athletics." The sunlight filtering through the backyard trees shot bands of light in Pat's eyes, offering me an unplanned psychological advantage. Pat was squinting and had raised his hand to cover his eyes as if he were saluting.

My name had already been typed in—showing the confidence that he had in the outcome of the preceding chat. The second line, empty at this point, was left blank for the amount. Pat reached down and scribbled in the amount of thirty-five thousand dollars—the figure that had repeatedly been used all day long. I'm sure Pat thought that by putting the amount on the empty line he would preempt any discussion about money. It almost worked.

In 1964, that kind of money was nothing to sneeze at, with or without chicken pox—which Pat was pretty sure he had had before. It represented several years' pay for most people and twice the cost of any house on our street. It was what the vice president of the United States was being paid. With money like that, I would be able to pay off the mortgage on my parents' house, buy them each a new car, and possibly have some money left over to invest in a business. A bonus like this was like winning the lottery.

Without much forethought, I said the first thing that came into my head. "Just one more thing," I said haltingly. Pat released his stare, shrugged his shoulder, and uttered a faintly audible puff of air from tightly pressed lips. He pushed back the chair with a scraping sound. Pat was thinking I was probably going to request a car or some other boyish extravagance. He would, of course, turn it down flatly, saying it "just wasn't in the budget."

"Okay," he said letting a smile wash across his face. "What do you have in mind?"

"Well, for one thing, the name is wrong," I said, and taking the pen, I wrote "Claude Edward Lockwood, Jr." in the space where my nickname was written. Then I said, "There's just one more thing right here," pointing to the space where the number $35,000 had been written. I put an oversized "1," in front of it. The additional numeral crowded the space designed for smaller numbers.

Pleased with myself, I turned the document around and slid it over toward Pat to witness. He went ashen. He didn't say anything for what seemed like an eternity. Maybe he didn't know what to say.

"What? Wait. What are you doing? We didn't agree on that number."

"We haven't agreed on any numbers yet," I corrected. Inwardly, I was squirming with anxiety, wondering whether or not I had just terminated any chance I might have of signing with the Athletics. "That's what it's going to take for me to see if that uniform shirt you brought with you today fits," I said, pointing to the number.

I had the sense that no one in corporate headquarters in Kansas City or Mr. Friday's plush leather-padded conference room would have dared such a stunt. Pat seemed to be at a loss for words and pushed back from the table like a child in timeout. He said, "I'm not authorized to spend that kind of money." The whole room got heavier.

"I need to call Charlie," he said, blotting his eyebrows.

"Let's call him," I replied, gesturing to the phone next to the fridge as I walked into the living room twenty feet away to give them a little privacy.

The phone call between Pat and Charlie was relatively short but expensive (a daytime long-distance call from Boston to Kansas City appeared on the next phone bill). At the end of the conversation, Pat's face seemed to brighten. I was hoping the gamble was worth the effort. Pat handed the phone to me. "He wants to speak to you."

"Hi, Mr. Finley, it's nice to talk with you too. Too bad you couldn't be here in Boston today."

Charlie asked one thing, "Why should I pay you that kind of money?"

I answered again without thinking, "Because I'll make you a winner."

The pause on the other end was dramatic and too long to have been planned.

"Put Pat back on the phone," Charlie said.

The next words that I heard from Pat were some of the most memorable I had ever heard. "Right. Okay. Will do, he'll be on a plane tomorrow. Sure, do you need to talk with him again?

Okay, right away." Putting the phone down, Pat turned to me with an expression of surprise and said, "Charlie said yes."

It flashed through my mind that on a quiet forgotten street in a small town outside of Boston, a young man's naivety, and maybe arrogance, had somehow outmaneuvered a top-notch negotiator bigwig from the biggest city in Kansas. The tables turned and an agreement was reached. The contract signing bonus suffered some reductions reflecting the addition of the Major League College tuition reimbursement plan. The major league salary was increased slightly, impacting the amount considered as the signing bonus. The terms of the negotiation were driven in part by the player's contract limitations and the conscious effort of the owners to limit the amount paid to young and unproven players coming into the league. In the end, though, a contract was signed for a mutually agreed upon amount, and the check was made out to the correct legal name. I became one of the highest-paid rookie players in baseball, a newly minted "bonus baby"—a name that I would grow to dislike, but appreciate, in the years to come.

I walked back to the bedroom where Dad and Mom were sequestered. I opened the door and said, "I signed. Come on out. Pat wants you to be the witness on the contract." Coming out of the bedroom, Dad reached the living room and the kitchen in less than ten steps. I could feel his excitement.

Pat spoke up, "This is an exceptional young man you have here, Claude, and we're delighted to have him on our team. I hope he will make a difference as soon as possible." Pat reached for a cigar in his coat pocket and offered it to Dad.

Grinning effusively, Dad said, "Well, so you're going to play for the A's." He was not, at this moment, aware of the terms of the contract. He picked it up and examined it. His eyes tumbled over the boilerplate language landing eventually to the page with the name and the amount. I could hear a gasp slip out of his mouth and see a smile creep over his face. He looked at me and muttered, "Well, well."

Pat Friday made two more phone calls, one to the Rawlings Glove Manufacturer, and another to the Hillerich & Bradsby bat manufacturer to arrange glove and bat contracts for me. The American League sales rep for Rawlings was scheduled to meet me in Cleveland to sign a contract, take some photos, and give me new equipment.

The Patriot Ledger, the local daily newspaper, came over to "capture the moment." Everyone in the family wanted to get into the photo. Elizabeth, red spots and all, appeared on the next day's sports page.

So I was under contract as a third baseman with a major league ball club willing to invest in young talent and, as it turned out, willing to be patient also. I would not make it as an infielder—an untimely basic training post with the army during the 1967 spring training season sacked my "assured" third base position with the A's in favor of Sal Bando—but would eventually come into my own as a pitcher. Charlie and I would have many things to talk about over the years as I was sent down, brought up, sold, traded, and released. In the end, it was Charlie who helped me make a major decision that pioneered my coveted role as a closing pitcher.

CHAPTER 7

AN UNWELCOMING WELCOME TO THE SHOW

AFTER SIGNING MY contract, things were completely out of my control. I was traveling at the speed of light. There was a lot to do and not much time to do it in. There were luggage and clothes to be bought and goodbyes to be said. The day after I signed, I said goodbye to my childhood adolescence and hello to the world of childish adults.

Charlie Finley wanted to showcase me around the league, starting with the road trip that the A's were on to Cleveland and Detroit. After that, I'd be sent down to the minor leagues for seasoning. I anxiously climbed aboard an airplane for the first time. Excitedly off on my own, I flew to Cleveland to meet a team full of big league baseball players, some whose bubble gum card I had.

When I joined the big league team, they were on a road trip in Ohio. They were solidly in last place, fifteen games out of first. As a team, they resembled a gaily dressed traveling troupe of clowns. The Athletics wore Old English-style A's on the left front of their Kelly-Green, Gaudy-Gold, and Wedding-Gown-White uniforms with an elephant dancing on a circus ball insignia on the right sleeve. It was rumored that the other teams in the league met the A's at the airport when they arrived to ensure that they got to the ballpark to play the games.

Years before the mainstreaming of Money Ball mania, Charlie Finley set out to grow the club generically from the minor leagues up. This nurturing required good coaches, and the A's had some of the best available. Gabby Hartnett and Luke Appling, both Hall of Famers and terrific instructors, were also both patient and wise. Gabby worked with the catchers and Luke with the infielders. Unfortunately, not all the coaches were so talented, generous, or gifted.

A coach named "Babe" was the opposite of the aforementioned gentlemen. Babe was not held in very high esteem by the baseball community in general, against whom he continued to hold a grudge, and he believed that he had been victimized by baseball brass after rumors spread regarding his association with drugs. He had grown into a surly man, twenty years older looking than his age, and he was just barely hanging on to his present job by doing two things that no one else wanted to do: throw batting practice and record the game on tape. He hated both jobs, but it meant a paycheck and a uniform, if only for a few hours before the game. Lately, his role with the team was limited to pitching batting practice because he stepped on the recording device. Regrettably, he was the first coach I got to meet up close and personal.

Babe heard through the grapevine that the front office had signed a kid out of Boston, a bonus baby. *Bunch of fools*, he probably thought. *Rookies are not worth the tobacco to spit on them,* he probably said to himself. Babe also didn't like Northerners, especially Bostonians.

Physically arriving into the big league meant going through a number of doors: doors leading to knowledge, doors leading to opportunity, and, most important, doors leading to self-awareness. The next door I opened was to the players entrance to Municipal Stadium. Once I went through that portal, my perception of baseball would change forever. While I would never lose my love for the game, it would take me time to deal with my disdain for some of its participants. This eye-opening door proved to be jaw-dropping troubling. The visiting players entrance was nothing more than a series of crowd control dividers leading into a dimly lit hallway with a sign that said "PLAYERS ONLY." The security guard gave me the once-over but let me in with minimal questioning. One door later I was standing in the middle of wooden lockers in a cramped dressing room. Moving tentatively, I literally bumped into "Doc," the clubhouse keeper. Doc had been in charge of the visiting clubhouse since the beginning of time. A cigarette butt was hanging out of his mouth as he loaded a bundle of towels into the wash, which was inconveniently located in the entrance hallway.

"Who are you?" Doc asked, not making eye contact. I offered a brief bio.

"Oh yea." he said. "They did say a kid might be coming in to dress for batting practice. Take that locker over there." He pointed a crooked finger toward a wood and screen mesh locker in the corner. Doc caught my eye and rotated his fingers, the "let's hurry up" signal.

I finished dressing in my A's uniform, pulled the belt tight, and took the cardboard packing material out of the cap, looking like a newly minted dollar bill. The back of my raglan shirt featured the number 8. I wondered if this number was mine or belonged to someone else. I couldn't worry about that right now. Doc pointed to the door that said "FIELD." It led directly to the visitor's dugout. I headed down the hallway that led to an opening lined with wood plank boards. I jumped the few steps up onto the field and excitedly landed in the big leagues.

A week ago, I was rushing back from my senior prom to get home before curfew. Today I was standing on a major league baseball field, on my own, with a little money in my pocket and a horde of reporters gathered wanting to meet and interview me. The world was spinning way too fast.

I was greeted by the media and took a few questions, but batting practice was not going to last too much longer, and I wanted to show my stuff.

"Yes, I was excited to be here . . . No, I did not think my bonus was excessive . . . Yes, I did realize there would be a lot of pressure on me to perform."

My eyes wandered as I listened to the sharp crack of the ball hitting the bat as it echoed in the empty stadium. I walked over toward the dugout steps to meet Eddie Lopat, the A's manager.

"Hello," Eddie said in a monotone, bored tone. He seemed to be concentrating partially on the batting practice and more intently on an attractive blonde near the first row.

"You Lockhart?"

"Lockwood," I corrected and stuck out my hand.

"Eddie Lopat," he said without shaking hands or looking up. He lifted one cheek of his rear and cut wind in my direction.

"Nice to meet you Mr. Lopat," I said, withdrawing my hand, embarrassed by his lack of civility. Running the corner of his eye over me with a wave of annoyance, a sneer formed on Eddie's lips, and he spit tobacco on the steps between us. It splashed into a well-established puddle with some outliers landing on my new white cleats. I looked down, cognizant of the second crass insult in as many seconds.

"We're all on a first-name basis here. Save your formal greetings for them teachers you had in high school back East. Here, I'm Eddie to you . . . same as everyone else. Now get out of my face. Grab your ass in that pretty new uniform over to the bat rack, pick one out of the pitcher's rack, the bat boys will show you where, and shag up there to the cage for a couple of swings before practice is over."

On a first-name basis already? I mused in mock humor. *Who would have guessed?* Obviously, the red carpet was not exactly being rolled out. I guessed that he had not read my press release this morning in the *Cleveland Plain Dealer*, or then again, maybe he had.

I did as I was told. The bat boy, about my age, was near the bat rack smoothing pine tar all over a towel. "Can I get a bat out of there . . . from the pitcher's section?" I asked and pointed to a group in the corner. "Sure," he said, "but if you break it, it will come out of your pay, and I'll get chewed out." "Coming out of my pay," now that's a curious phrase. It came to me that I was getting paid to play a game I'd gladly do for free. It also came to me that I needed to gain some wisdom very soon.

I stepped out onto the field with a bat made for bunting and was swallowed up by the enormity of the stadium and the moment. A little girl about ten was hanging over the dugout railing trying to get an autograph from any player that might happen by her. She held out her ball as I passed. "Are you any-one?" she asked. That seemed to be the question of the day, and I didn't really know the answer.

On road trips, the visiting team takes batting practice after the home team and the utility players, aka schrubbeanies, take batting practice after the starters. It's all very tightly choreo-graphed and time is limited. Five other players were waiting their turn to take their swings, five swings the first round, three the second, and then base hits . . . the only swings that they would probably get that day. Time was not on my side. The team was already halfway through their pregame practice. The utility players knew there were only a few swings left on the time clock and resented having to share them with anyone, let alone a non-roster player and a rookie to boot.

I was anxious to take my first swings in a big-league ball-park even though they were ceremonial. They represented a rite of passage for me. This was my new home and the place where I now belonged.

"Go ahead, jump in there. You get five pitches this round," said one of the players.

I flashed back to all the perfect swings I had made in my basement practicing, all the successful swings against All-Star high school pitchers. This was the first day of my professional career, time to show off my power and make a few heads turn. I couldn't wait for the first ball to land over the left field wall and watch the reaction of the other players to my effortless power and perfect swing.

****

I turn the corner at the cage by pivoting around the corner of the metal pipe of the batting cage and do a little two-step into the batter's box nearest to me. BP is practice time. Players gather around the cage, put their feet up on the wheels, and lean on the cross bars. I feel like a monkey in a cage. I know I am being showcased here, and I want to put on a good show.

The first pitch is way inside, surprising since the batting practice pitcher's sole job is to goose in strikes. I take it, but I have to dance my feet a little in the dirt. The batting practice pitcher, Babe, is glaring in at me as I wait for my second chance to impress.

Someone around the cage yells, "You got four more Rook."

The location of the second pitch is worse. It hits me in the middle of the back. I fall down in the dirt next to home plate with a thud. This is crazy, I think. The BP pitcher must be getting tired or something after throwing so many pitches. I jump up and brush myself off.

"Swing the bat, man, we ain't got much more time," someone cries from outside the cage. I hear a few chuckles. The third pitch from Babe is more like a dart thrown at a bull's eye. It is straight,

carries a message, and arrives as aimed. It hits me hard. This one stings and, had I not ducked, could have caused a concussion. It glances off my shoulder. In the dirt again I understand now the beanings are deliberate. I opt to forgo the next couple of swings to let the pain and indignity subside and to settle my mind.

Laughter erupts from the players standing around the cage. They all seem to be enjoying the strange sideshow. As I exit the cage, I shout at Babe, a total stranger to me in every way. "Throw the fucking ball over the plate, meat," slips out of my mouth. Undoubtedly it's a bush comment, but it comes from my confusion and naivety. The word "meat" is a derogatory term for a pitcher and indicates that their pitches are meatballs, soft and easy to hit. I have never used that term with anyone, and it surprises me that the words are coming out of my mouth.

Babe glares back and shouts, "I've got your meat right here," and he grabs his crotch. "Get your candy-ass back in there. You get two more pitches, and I ain't done with you. You can count, can't you, even if you can't hit." His voice crackles in rage.

****

Babe, a large square man, a Neanderthal dressed in a baseball uniform thirty pounds past his prime, was taking time to collect his composure. He was snorting like an escaped bull from the pen and pacing around the mound mumbling to himself. This looked like a chapter from a Civil War book. I could feel his anger and self-righteousness. One of the coaches ran out to calm him down. It's the first time in anyone's memory that a batting practice pitcher ever got a visit from a pitching coach.

The next hitter due up, Larry Stahl, was just coming back from the disabled list after being out with a shoulder injury. He yelled to Babe, "You hit me, asshole, and I'll hide all the beer in the clubhouse." Everyone howled, and Babe seemed to loosen up a little too.

After the four other utility players took their five pitches, it would be my turn again. Two pitches only, and if the second is a base hit, I get to stand in for another swing, but it has to be a clean hit.

****

I get a strike this time but foul it into the batting cage. The second pitch I hit pretty well, up the middle, a clean single. As I stand in to get the extra pitch I deserve, I hear Babe yell, "Get your ass out of there. The shortstop would gobble that weak shit up in this here league." Everyone laughs again at my expense. Batting practice is over for me. I am relieved to see it end. It is not at all like what I have always envisioned and definitely nothing like what I expected.

****

After hitting practice, the visiting team takes infield practice. The coach hits balls to the outfielders, who throw them into the bases, and then to the infielders who, in turn, throw them to first, then second, and then to home as if fielding a bunt.

Ed Charles was the A's starting third baseman, and I was being touted in the papers as the third baseman of the future. A black man with silky moves and an easy disposition, his

teammates called him "Easy Ed" because he made everything look so easy, effortless, and graceful. He had power
and a sweet swing that sent the ball to all fields. Ed and
I stood on the infield dirt near third base together in an
awkward silence.

Having witnessed the batting practice beatdown, Ed empa-
thized and grinned, remembering his own first days in professional baseball. "How you doing, young man?" Ed asked.

"I guess I'm okay," I replied, my shoulders drooping.

"Don't pay Babe no mind. He's just mad at everyone.
Thinks everyone's against him. Needs his Mamma to smack
him upside the head. Oh and he ain't no coach. He's just the
BP pitcher." The conversation released some of my tension.
I let out a long overdue exhale.

"Where you from?" Ed asked.

"Just outside Boston. A little town called Norwood."
I answered.

"That might be a problem in these parts. Lots of these
tobacco-spitting Southerners ain't fond of Yankees. Probably
still fighting the ambush at Shiloh. I come from Florida," Ed
said. "Born and raised down there with them alligators. Man,
does it get hot in the summer. Hot and sticky, like being in a
sauna all the time." He fielded one of the throws from center
field and underhanded a perfect strike to second base.

I liked Ed. True to his name, he was easy to talk to. He had
soft hands and seemed able to handle any ball without a question. "Hey listen . . . this shit you're going through . . . will
probably last only . . . a couple of games but no longer, unless

you let it get under your skin or if you really screw up. It's part of being accepted here. You've got to earn your own turf." He fielded another ball and smoothed a throw to first . . . again a perfect strike.

"Do you know if you're going to stay with us or ship out somewhere?" he asked, totally unconcerned that we both played the same position.

"I think I'm going down to Burlington in a day or so. I think that's A Ball, but I'm not sure."

"That sounds about right. Yep, that be deep in the bush leagues," Ed said, taking a backhanded throw from right field and popping a fake tag on the imaginary runner. A big wide smile said he had the out at third.

"Ain't none of my business, but while you're here, try to keep your feelings inside . . . Don't let the shit-eaters bother you. Everyone gets the same treatment when they first come up. You'll have to earn respect by hitting, not talking. Simple. Play good, and they'll be your best friend. Play shitty, and they treat you like you got some disease or something."

Charles crept closer to home plate, like a cat stalking a mouse, fielded a tricky hop, and flipped it to first base. Ed's style was to creep in towards the hitter each and every pitch— his signature move. He fielded another ball, yelling over his shoulder, "I'm just going to take one more ball and leave the rest for you, young'n." The ball took an impossibly bad hop right at the very end. Ed was too quick for it, fielded it without a problem, and snapped a running strike to first as he glided in toward the dugout, leaving me alone at third.

I completely missed the first ground ball. The ball must have hit the same impediment in the infield as the grounder to Ed. It slid right through my legs and rolled out into left field. The coach at home plate quickly hit another to me right away before anyone noticed. This ball hit off the side of my new glove and rolled towards the foul line. Frustrated, I picked it up and threw it too hard to first. The third grounder was better; I scooped it with two hands and threw it confidently to the visibly annoyed first baseman.

Showcase over and my first-day jitters on display, I jogged into the locker room to meet up with the rest of my new "friends." The locker room was as small as the stadium was big and permeated with the aroma of Raid. The lockers were barely wide enough to fit a stool in front.

As luck would have it, my locker was near Babe's. He was still fuming about his personal problem with rookies, his misfortune compared to their good fortune. On his way for a beer, he passed my stool and bent over and said, "Wish I had stuck it in your rookie ear. Do you have any idea where your candy-ass is?"

If the question was geographic in nature, in truth, I might have had a problem with the answer. Given the ire and sarcasm that was spitting out of the corners of his mouth, I guessed that Babe was aiming at a more philosophic response.

"Where am I?" I replied mockingly, reflexively.

When I left home less than twenty-four hours ago, I knew I would have to make it on my own. I'd have to fight my own battles. I would not be accepted into this game until I earned respect. But I was confident in my talent, and I would not be belittled for my age or where I came from. I did not understand Babe's emotional instability, but I knew this was some kind of test being administered in public view. Dignity and honor were at stake. I was not going to back down, not today or ever. Babe was expecting me to timidly back down, but instead I stood up.

"This here place belongs to professionals not the likes of you," Babe growled, still in his underwear and showing a mid-section girth much in need of a few more situps and few less beers. He stepped closer. The players in near proximity spun around smelling an argument, hoping for more. Tension had been mounting in the locker room because of the team's poor on-field performance. They all needed something to break the jinx. Players craned their necks around the sharp corners of the lockers.

I assumed that civil camaraderie would come with wearing the same uniform, but apparently, sixty minutes in the green-and-gold were not enough to cement that bond. Babe was tightening his fists as he pushed one of the stools aside for better access. His nostrils flared. His gray hair lay flat on the side of his head. To me, he looked burnt out, but nevertheless, I decided I better take him seriously.

Babe swore and moved to a more combative stance. He slapped his own stool to the floor. His complexion dimmed from white-gray to ashen. I widened my stance too, thinking, "Is this guy really going to take a swing at me. For what? Why?"

"Yea, Rookie. Why don't you just get up from here and go back where you came from!" Babe said working himself into a rage again. I let my eyes follow the overturned stool. I was very much an unproven rookie in this surrounding. Looking at me with contempt, he saw a pathetic, incompetent rookie, not worth a bonus or even deserving of a uniform. He emitted a single, guttural noise like an animal snort, triggering an adrenaline surge from his nervous system. He drew back to make a swing.

"Don't do that, old man," I said reflexively. Again my words were not well chosen and, like before, only enraged him more. Babe had kept his resentment inside for way too long. Now he was in attack mode. His fists en route, he lost his balance, undisciplined in this type of physical behavior, and stumbled. The blow landed mostly on my shoulder. I saw it coming and ducked towards the towel bin.

This was my first fight ever but as I would soon find out, not my last. I was in survival mode. All eyes in the room were harvesting the show. I punched back with a right. I felt a swoop of elation as we surged backward. Babe was on one knee near his locker. He knew he'd been hit, and he knew he missed with his best chance. Enraged, he stopped to collect his thoughts from the impact and design a counter. This fight was far from over.

Babe gathered himself, still kneeling, and noticed the assortment of extra bats stored handle-up next to the wall. He grabbed one, scraping his elbow, losing his balance for a second time. His mouth was distorted, and he tried to gain some leverage. The irony of the situation was palpable. I was a rookie and on display. Really. Here's an old batting practice coach trying to make a serious mark on my head and career. I pounced on him, getting a knee into his chest, smothering the fight.

"What the hell is going on?" yelled Luke Appling, one of the coaches. Both Babe and I were on the ground panting for air, absurdly dressed in our underwear. A pool of blood was dripping under the overturned stool.

"Break it up. Break it up. What the fuck is going on? Why are you guys all sitting around watching them fight?"

The fight was over. I was back up on my stool and out of breath, shocked that I had been in my first street fight. I stood up and caught a glimpse of a mirror on the wall about ten feet away. I didn't recognize my own reflection. This was certainly not the welcome I imagined as I embarked on my career as a big leaguer.

****

Mulling over the events of the day, I was mortified that I had been so disrespected by people I had assumed I should offer respect, but mollified that I had withstood the ordeal and maintained my self-respect. Having been king of the hill for so long, I was shocked at my new status of persona non grata. Still, I didn't want to make more of this incident than it deserved. This childish "Babe" evidently had a problem that needed professional intervention. He mistakenly thought that I would be an easy target for his wrath. On the upside, I believed I had found an on-field mentor in Ed Charles and an off-field protector in Luke Appling. Having been challenged as a rookie, I responded like a veteran. It was evident that from here on out I was going to have to fight for what was mine. Nothing was going to be handed to me.

CHAPTER 8
THE BOONIES: BURLINGTON, IOWA, 1964

AFTER A FEW days, time that actually seemed like months with the big club, I shipped out as planned to the Burlington Bees in the Midwest League, located directly in the middle of the country, during a very hot, dry summer. The short flight took all day with stops in Toledo and Waterloo before a harrowing landing at Burlington's Municipal Airport. After my reception in Cleveland, I couldn't wait for what was in store for me in the Bees' clubhouse. I was a long way from home and going farther.

The roster changes that preceded my arrival did little to help me fit into my new surroundings. Infielder Jim Pamlanye, a charismatic clubhouse comedian, was placed on the injured reserve list to make room for me, most likely a sign signaling the end of Jim's career. For all new players, the pathway onto the field leads past someone who is already there. That's just how it works. It doesn't make everyone happy, but I, at this point, didn't expect a welcome wagon from new teammates.

The five banks of lights thirty feet high on the wooden stanchions served the field these last twenty years both as game time illumination when on and guardians of hope and promise for tomorrow's game when off. The high lights were turned off, and a handful of lower floodlights had taken their place. Each had a swarm of bugs of every description attacking them as if they were a strange form of decomposing food. What light there was struggled in the chaos, spitting out a din of small particles across the gravel parking lot, like fog enveloping a lighthouse.

My taxi contributed to the dust as it pounded into view, about 11:30 pm, long after the game was over. I joined the team just as they were heading out on a road trip to Des Moines in a cramped car caravan. No bus for this team. The first car carried the manager, the next game's starting pitcher, the player leading the club in batting, and the driver, aka trainer. The next three cars were filled with the remaining players in a loose arrangement of friendships and roommates.

In the weeks that followed, I hit like a seventeen-year-old just out of high school, which was precisely what I was also. I definitely did not hit like one of the best prospects in the country, which I was, of course. The feeling among the coaching staff was that I just needed to see more pro pitching and make the adjustment to the breaking ball.

With expectations weighing heavily on my shoulders, it was a constant battle to remain focused on improving my game and ignoring the hype. "I try not to fall into that trap of listening to the negative things in my own head," I said. "You'll hear it, whether you like it or not, but the less you try to put that pressure on yourself, the better it is for you." In the minor leagues, every day and every ballgame is a constant audition. Day in and day out you're trying to impress someone—maybe just one person, maybe a scout, maybe another manager. Getting to the Bigs has a number of different routes. This route that I was taking seemed anything but express.

By the first of August, I was really pressing. The team traveled to Decatur, Illinois, for a three-game set against the Decatur Commodores. The trip was made a little easier this time as the team upgraded travel accommodations from the cramped station wagons to a vintage school bus. Beer flowed freely, and the outrageous antics of the quirkier clubhouse clowns eased some of my self-imposed anxiety.

Most minor league teams conjure up promotions to entice paying customers into the seats. The owners of the Commodores franchise had tried pregame jugglers, cow-milking contests, and a farmer's day to lure in the locals. Not much seemed to work. On that night, they were experimenting with a different kind of drawing card. They hired an imposter player, named Max Patkin, to coach third base during the middle innings of the night game.

Max Patkin had been a ballplayer, but his playing days were over. After an injury curtailed his minor league baseball career, Patkin joined the Navy and pitched for a service team. He had a camel hump in the middle of his fastball and a watch-out at the end of his curveball. His record was not in the least bit funny, but he was.

As the story goes, during one of the service games Joe DiMaggio homered off of him and, in mock anger, Patkin threw his glove down and followed DiMaggio around the bases threatening him with glaringly ineffective, fake punches, and the antics of a deranged man. The fans were delighted, and Max had an idea for a new career that would keep him in uniform for years. Max retired from the service and repackaged his career as a baseball imposter, a clown, a joker, an actor . . . all wrapped up in baseball garb.

Max became the Clown Prince of Baseball. He was a barnstorming vaudevillian baseball coach playing in minor league stadiums throughout the United States and Canada. His face contorted like playdough into a thousand expressions. He was thin "like a zipper," as one player remarked. He wore a baggy old wool uniform two sizes too big with a question mark on the back instead of a number. His ball cap was always askew. He had his head in the stands looking for the ladies before, after, and mostly during the games.

On this particular evening, Max had been hired by the Commodores to handle the third base coaching duties for two innings for both the home and visiting team, even though he was paid by the home team. His main skit consisted of giving hilarious signs, outrageous antics, crotch rubs, pointing and dirt throwing, and harassing everyone close to him on the field. In addition, he would throw his hat down in the dirt when a player missed a pitch and completely lose it if someone struck out or, heaven forbid, hit into a double play. The people howled at his antics, as did the players.

In between routines, Max came over to the visiting dugout for some water. He sat down next to me, and I edged away from him far enough that our uniforms wouldn't touch. Max scooted towards me in acknowledgment of my evasive move. "What's up good lookin'?" he said to me as if he was trying to pick me up in a bar. "Do you come here often? Do you come at all?" The bench players fell over laughing.

I was horrified that somehow I was being drawn into his ridiculous antics, but I had nowhere to go to hide. Uncomfortable and wishing I was somewhere else, I sensed that Max was edging, as he played to the crowded dugout. Max grinned like the Cheshire cat. He was missing a lower left tooth.

"Hi Big Boy," he said mimicking Mae West. "Didn't I see you in the last city I played?" I was not sure what to do or say.

"You know rook," he said looking me over again, "it's tough to stay in baseball when you don't have any talent." The comment got a roar from the other players on the bench. I found myself laughing too.

"Hey listen, kid. I want you to do me a favor and play along with a couple gags next inning?" I shrugged knowing I really didn't have an option.

"Great," said Max as he rolled his eyes for the others to see. Again, the laughter was deafening.

I was the leadoff batter in the top of the next inning. Max was ensconced down at the third base coaching box. Max began with some ridiculous gyrations more suited for a striptease pole than for a ballfield. He was grinding and clawing at his crotch. In a strange kind of way, it was really quite funny. Suddenly he broke into prayer. He crossed himself, looked toward the heaven, and knelt down in the dirt coaching box facing the third base bleachers. He was praying with hands tightly clasped together, ardently petitioning for me to get a hit.

The pitcher delivered "ball one" according to the ump, who was fully complicit with Max's shenanigans. Max started the signs all over again. His routine, which included a complete whipping of both shoulders, pants, shirt, and cap, this time ended with the middle finger. I stood at the plate and watched him in fear and amazement.

Max called, "Timeout, ump," and retrieved his wallet out of the back pocket of his very baggy pants. He thumbed through the handful of bills and came up with a few dollars. He was delighted with a few dollars; any amount would make the crowd laugh. He showed the wad to the crowd, who began to egg him on. He slowly walked toward me in the batter's box. A well-watered fan in the nearest box seats yelled, "Go ahead Rook, take the money. You've earned it." A little boy next to him couldn't understand what was going on. The idea of offering a bribe to a player was a completely foreign concept, and Max was going to milk it for all it was worth.

Feeling hopelessly trapped in this skit I edged toward the back of the box hoping to avoid any further attention. The pitcher threw another ball. Max had the crowd eating out of his hand. With a conspiratorial look on his face Max got to home plate and gestured for me to take a look at the wad of money he held in his hands—clearly meant as a bribe and enticement to get a base hit on the next pitch.

I declined by waving my hands in a no-thank-you kind of motion over the money, the move appearing more like a blessing than a refusal. My actions, unintended and uninspired, were in many ways more comical than Max anticipated. He was slinking around behind me, trying to hide the money. Max appeared to be very upset to be publicly rejected with just a wave of the hand. He offered me a few more dollars from his other pocket, thinking I might capitulate if he upped the ante. I shook my head "no."

Looking forlorn now, he stooped his head and started to walk back to the third base coaching box, kicking the dirt in disgust. But he stopped halfway with an idea. Turning, he walked back to home plate to make the same offer to the umpire, who let him go through a process of actually counting the money in his wallet. However, in the end, the ump also turned him down. The fans were going crazy.

After what seemed like a twenty-minute intermission, the pitcher, who was also laughing at Max and me, delivered ball two. With the second ball in a favorable count, Max acted as if his prayers had been answered, and he offered a moment of thanks to the Almighty in a not so private prayer service. Next Max took out glasses from the same pocket as the billfold and offered them to both the ump and me.

This whole thing was too funny to believe unless, of course, you're the one standing in the batter's box. Scene two was taking more time off the play clock. I longed to either get on base or retreat back into the safety of the dugout. The third pitch was close to the strike zone, so I took a swing and singled it to center.

Max could not believe our success. His ecstatic behavior included animated high fives along the left field dugout with the fans and throwing his hat into the air. I thought first base might not be far enough away to be safe.

Max began to give me signs from the coaching box. As if in answer, the first base coach was giving signs back toward Max. Similar gestures, similar whips, and identical tipping of the hat were coming from both sides. Signs were going back and forth. Signs were coming fast and furious. None of them meant anything. I looked at Max and then the first base coach, who appeared to be mimicking and mocking Max with the bogus signs. Max's face contorted in mock anger. He acted agitated. He threw his hat. The first base coach, in turn, threw his hat. Max put his hands on his hips. The first base coach did the same. Clearly, Max was being mocked. An argument erupted one hundred and twenty-five feet apart, literally in sign language. The crowd went wild.

Max was a crowd-pleaser, and he was on a roll. He knew it. Unwillingly, I was playing a part in this hit comedy show. The time allotted for Max's little performance was running down. The real game had to go on sooner or later, but Max had one more prank up his threadbare sleeve.

The next two batters struck out on bad pitches, one so wild I managed to take second base. Max belittled them with facial expressions of disbelief and pantomimes of exasperation. With two outs, he appeared to be desperate to score a run. He was pulling out all the stops. He called a loud "timeout" and without waiting for the umpire to respond, took a few steps toward second base where I was standing.

Max motioned me to come over and meet him for a conference, somewhere on the third base-side of shortstop. Animated with excited gestures, he whispered to me, "When we separate, you go to third, and I'll go to second."

He was suggesting a stealthy slow walking motion as part of this base-stealing caper. The heist began as orchestrated when we separated—Max walking slowly to second base, head down sulking, and I walking slowly to third, a distance of about ten feet. The shortstop and third baseman were standing together laughing in short left field, certainly not wanting to be dragged into it. They were too far away to do anything, even if they could figure out what was up. By the time the infielders and the pitcher realized what was going on, the runner switch had occurred and a base was stolen without breaking a sweat. I was standing on third. Max calmly stood on second with his hands on his hips.

The umpire at third, looking at the bag as if there was a close play, said "safe" in a dramatic way and motioned the safe sign. Max looked more surprised than anyone. How could he have gotten so mixed up and walked to the wrong base?

The umpires were in on the plot, but the managers were not. Now an argument between the managers and the three umps ensued out on the field near shortstop. Max was in his glory, having wormed his way into the middle of it. To the fans, this was better than Abbott and Costello's "Who's on First?" routine. The managers and the umps formed a circle, and they all began to scream at each other. Max was initially on the outside, but he ducked under the circle and inserted himself into the middle. This happened two or three times like a scrum in rugby.

Eventually, the whole ridiculous scene was over. The fans standing in the bleachers were bent over with pains in their sides from laughing. The electric light on the scoreboard lit up. Evidently, time was never requested or given, so the whole meeting between Max and me was "in play." The scoring on the play went as a stolen base, albeit a walking stolen base, my first in professional baseball.

The season slowly fizzled out with a split in Decatur. I got a hit in my last at-bat and earned some accolades from my teammates by scoring a savvy fielding play on a swinging bunt in the seventh inning to save a run, a personal triumph ending a trying period of adjustment. Most of my teammates were taking some off time and heading back to winter quarters in their hometowns. An excited few were talking about going to the Dominican Republic or Puerto Rico for winter ball. I had not been invited to play on a winter ball team.

I left the park and went back to my boarding house to pick up my personal belongings. I stopped in for a final goodbye to my clairvoyant landlady, who offered one of her unassuming zingers: "Seems to me you could use the offseason to figure out what you want from your life. It looks to me like you're running away from something. You'll never find what you're looking for if you don't have a clear picture of where you're going to or worry that someone might be catching up to you." She stopped and looked at me. I nodded, deep in thought inside my own skin. "Seems to me that the only truth is the words you say to yourself. The only way home is the direction of hope and promise. And the only people you can trust are the ones who ain't lookin' for anything back." I shrugged and forced a smile and went up the back stairs to finish packing up.

****

I was the bonus baby with expectations weighing heavily on my shoulders. It was a constant battle to remain focused on improving my game and ignoring the hype. I knew I had to turn things around but had no clue how to lighten up and, for that matter, loosen my grip. The situation was baffling and getting worse. In the words of the players, I was "pressing." I knew that I had lost something and didn't quite know how to get it back. I had spent the summer trying harder and harder but to no avail.

CHAPTER 9

RUNNING ON EMPTY: BRADENTON, FLORIDA, 1965

THE 1965 KANSAS City Athletics team was comprised of an eclectic bunch composed of old pros battling time and new blood battling acne. Which group might catch fire and ignite the revitalization of the franchise was a million-dollar question for management, and the answer would, as it turned out, take years to unfold.

As franchises go, there are many ways of building a winning team, though all seem to be expensive. The path the Athletics chose was to go with an overload of young players. They would keep seven unproven teenagers on the roster—Don Buschhorn, Tom Harrison, Catfish Hunter, Rene Lachemann, Blue Moon Odom, John Sanders, and me—and try to balance things out with eight experienced veterans over the age of thirty like Ed Charles, Moe Drabowsky, and Don Mossi. The combination of personalities made things kind of nutty.

Spring training was held in Bradenton, Florida, a sand strip that would become gold along Florida's west edge in about twenty-five years. In the '60s, though, it was a warm flat place for walking sticks and portable oxygen machines. A town of tall palms, it was far from what it is today.

Bradenton was predominantly pink—full of pink stucco houses, a large pink hotel on the beach area, and pink fleshy people waddling in and out of shopping malls. A peachy patina shone off the majority of sunbirds who swarmed around the ball field. Amidst all this pink clashed the gaudy gold-and-green Athletics uniform on the red-faced rookies running sprints.

The spring training stadium was pretty empty at this hour in the late afternoon, except for the "scrubbinnies," a group of non-starters, many with numbers too large to fit comfortably on their uniforms. Sprints and stretches were underway in the outfield grass near the clubhouse. The afternoon thunderstorms were coming.

Willie Thompson's billowing voice could be heard from the clubhouse porch all over the neighborhood. He was clubhouse man, in the middle of everything. Out on the old turn-of-the-century wooden porch that wrapped around the clubhouse like a cummerbund on a Confederate uniform, he was hanging out socks to dry. Willie had a big round face and hands like flank steaks. He was of indeterminable age, greying a bit around the temples. He might have been old in years, but he was all kid at heart and deathly afraid of snakes. He'd squeal like a banshee when we'd chase him with a garden snake from one of the lockers, the epidemy of eternal youth with playful dark eyes. He had a toothy smile with summer teeth, "soma here and soma there," as he used to cackle, followed by a howl of self-pleasure.

It was getting late in the day. The crowd of players had long thinned out and only a few stragglers lingered with Willie on the porch where he had everyone in stitches with stories about chasing alligators and something called "pootang." Crows and maven birds made their way through the home plate stands flapping and squawking to each other, their eerie cries echoing in the empty ballpark. The grounds crew was out starting to mow the grass and groom the infield dirt for tomorrow's practice.

I was still running sprints, left field to center, walking back and doing it again. In the mid-afternoon March sun, I was sweating, soaked, and questioning my decision to wear a wool/dacron blend long-sleeve sweatshirt. I was in a zone, focused solely on planting one foot ahead of another, wondering what the next few weeks would bring. Ostensibly getting in shape by running sprints, I was really running to impress. "Be the last one to leave the field," Luke Appling, Chicago Hall of Fame shortstop and Athletics coach, had told me when I first got to spring camp. "And stay out of them fights," he added. It was good advice, and so I kept on, doggedly putting one foot in front of another.

Wind sprints, like on-off switch running, are a spring training formality. At eighteen I was already in great shape, but all players run wind sprints and, in doing so, stand guard over long-held baseball tradition—managers and coaches stand around and watch players run. I was running for my life and hoping to be noticed.

I had just finished sprint number twenty. "Hi," a voice said. "I'm Jesse." The voice, all friendly, right next to me in an almost empty field, startled me. My head jolted as I turned sharply to view my outfield companion.

"Still running, kid?" Jesse seemed to have just appeared. He passed ghostly quick and then slowed so that I could catch up. I turned to walk back with him, two strangers meeting in a place where strangers aren't allowed.

Jesse started talking out of the blue as if we knew each other. He talked faster than he ran, all the way back from center field. His speech was purposeful, different, and very chatty. Strange, but Jesse didn't have a uniform on. He was outfitted head to toe in Adidas gear—a jogging top, gray with a funny logo, and long jogging bottoms, which were creased like they just were unwrapped from cellophane. But his sneakers told a different story. These were filled with miles of memories. I wanted to ask him what he was doing on the field, if he was a manufacturer's rep for Adidas, but I couldn't get a word in.

"What do you think about when you run?" he asked.

"What?" I replied.

"What do you think about out here doing this?" he clarified.

Panting and now pondering in equal measures, I hadn't thought much about what I thought about. I don't think. And, for that matter, I don't talk when I run. "I just sort of run," I said.

"No. I mean on the inside," he continued. "What are you trying to be?" I was trying to gasp for a little of the Florida ozone and not really use the body parts needed for this request.

"Be?" I asked out loud. "I'm not trying to *be* anything. I'm just hoping this uniform, this number 8, will make it onto this year's opening day roster."

"Hey listen, kid," he replied, knowing instinctively that I needed some guidance and further information to Zen such ponderousness. "Boss sent me here to work with you and a couple of the other players to help you run better." The Boss was Charlie Finley, owner of the Kansas City Athletics. I looked at him harder.

"I'm here to see if I could make you faster, steal more bases, and catch more flies. That kind of stuff," he continued looking back at me, letting the words seep in.

Jesse was a black man with owl-round eyes and darker patches under both like he hadn't been allowed to sleep. His pupils, narrow in the Florida heat, were intense and piercing. He had pale brown skin and high cheekbones. He looked, at first glance, to be in his mid-fifties, but he was sinewy and muscular. Jesse and I reached the chalk line together and turned to run another sprint into center field, side by side in imaginary lanes. We turned again and accelerated. I was charging ahead full speed, and Jesse was jogging, but we arrived there at the same time.

"What's your name, again?" I asked. "Jesse," he said again and held out his hand. I realized then that I was shaking hands with history. "You're Jesse Owens," I said, beginning to recognize his face from *Sports Illustrated* articles. "Yep, one and the same, and Charlie sent me here to see if I can't make you faster."

In the 1936 Olympic Games, Jesse Owens was the colorful face of competition for Adolf Hitler's boasts of Aryan supremacy and the domination of Hitler's ideal white, European athletes. Owens won a total of four gold medals at the Summer Olympic Games. Stunned, Hitler angrily left the stadium before the laurel leaves crowned the winners. No handshakes came from the Führer, but the other German athletes embraced Owens and the spectators furiously chanted his name.

Jesse noted the recognition in my eyes and offered confirmation. "You've probably heard the whole story, but I just have to tell you that monster wouldn't shake my hand," he said, speaking about Hitler, as we walked back the second time, "and it really infuriated me.

"I knew he wasn't going to shake my hand after the ceremonies, so I just looked up at him, made eye contact, and nodded defiantly. He just got up and left."

Now the legendary Olympian, Jesse Owens was running with me—just the two of us side by side. His voice was soft and knowing, like a grandfather reading a book in front of the fire. Clearly, he was here to talk. "You know when I run I always run towards, not away," he instructed. "Running away is all about fear. Running towards is about courage." His sentences chopped off in places, like he spoke from a summons delivered, with parts of the pages missing.

Jesse said, "Speed comes from the heart, kid. It travels like shock waves to the feet, to the brain, and to the hands. Every part of you has got to find the speed I'm talking about, not just your feet," he reflected, slightly unfocused, engrossed in a memory that spilled over the corners of his mouth with an alacrity of pride, protest, and frustration. "You become fast by determination and by believing.

"Anyone ever told you that you run like a duck?" he scolded me. "You need to keep your head still. You need to bend more from the waist and don't do that to your neck. Run like you feel that the ground is on fire and you don't want to be touching it." His voice trailed off. He clapped his hands as if to signal the end of the conversation and the end of his wisdom for me. He was called back into the locker room by Willie and trotted off. Unfortunately, I never had the chance to speak with Jesse Owens again, but I never forgot his advice.

Florida was heating up as spring training edged closer and closer to opening day. The intensity of the heat matched my demeanor the day after my encounter with Jesse. The temperature on the field surrounded the players like hot fog as we headed out for morning calisthenics. I felt unusually happy, light-footed, and eager to get to work, having been instructed and empowered by a world-renowned track legend.

Over the past twenty-four hours, I had chewed on Jesse's words. The unapologetic tone of his voice let me know he expected something special of me. All in all, it was the perfect message for a hungry eighteen-year-old looking for a way to stand out in a game filled with talent. His last words to me resonated strongly: "You have to take it, 'cause they won't give it to you."

As I got to the ballpark, I stared at the lineup card taped to the dugout wall. In bold print, my name was listed, playing third base, batting seventh. My heart jumped a beat.

****

INSIGHT PITCH

During the first inning, I watch closely as my teammates approach the plate. From the edge of the dugout, I stalk my opponent. His fastball definitely has life, but his control seems a little off. Dissecting his delivery with men on base, I gauge how high he lifts his leg. I time his windup. He walks two but gets out of the inning unscathed.

I finally get my chance in the second inning and hit a sharp single off left field on the third pitch. Running to first, I feel electricity in my steps and the intensity of dark oval eyes in the stands following my every move. I round the back of the base with light, quick steps, barely touching the ground. Slowing and stopping about ten feet towards second base, I feel Jesse's presence as if he's the first base coach. I stretch out a lead from first five then six feet, feeling the spikes press against my arches. My shoelaces stretch across my instep from the pressure inside my shoes.

Shifting back and forth on the balls of my feet like a fighter, I bide my time, waiting for the pitcher to make his move. Ball one in the dirt. I immediately make a decision. I'm going on the next pitch. I wait for a second to let the pitcher come to a stretch. The pitcher looks over. I chuckle to myself and keep my mouth open so that I won't blink. He has absolutely no chance in this little contest of ours. He makes the mistake of not throwing over and, as he lifts his foot to go to home plate, I lift mine. His right foot digs as his left knee comes higher and higher. I'm committed now and, like a shot of a starter's pistol, I'm off. In my ears, I hear Jesse say, "Go get it."

My lead arm, the right arm, pulls at the air like a rope pulling second base toward me, and I twist and bend, staying low as long as possible. I don't want to spend any time at all on the ground. Just like Jesse said, "the dirt feels on fire." Pushing my legs down from the air . . . faster and faster down and up from the burning ground . . . quick up and then down again. My palms open, my fingers spread, and my shoulders lead me forward.

I see an empty second base. The steal is a surprise. The last thing a veteran catcher would think is that a rookie, in his first plate appearance, would try a stunt like stealing on his own early in the count. There's no one at second. It's mine for the sheer will of taking it. I say to myself "go." I own it. As fast as I can, using the techniques Jesse and I worked on yesterday, I'm there. Sliding straight in with a pop-up slide. Safe. There's no play. A wave of appreciation floats my way. Cheers. Applause. Shouts. And when they all calm down and settle back into their seats, I hear an exuberant pair of hands, the hands of a champion, clapping rhythmically near the home base side of the field.

CHAPTER 10
KANSAS CITY HERE I COME, 1965

SPRING TRAINING ENDED and, at the ripe old age of eighteen years and seven months, I was officially a Kansas City Athletics Major League Baseball player.

Catfish Hunter was my road trip roommate throughout the 1965 season. Reared in Hertford, North Carolina, he rolled over every vowel he ever spoke. Jim "Catfish" Hunter was a character straight out of a Mark Twain novel. I first met Catfish in the Manatee River Hotel in Bradenton. He stuck his hand out to shake. I went to shake it and was immediately unnerved. I couldn't believe he had six fingers. I asked him if his sixth finger helped him pitch? Jim smiled a boyish grin and answered, "No. But that extra little finger helps when I jack off." As the immature teenagers we both were, we laughed in unison at an oft-told old joke. Catfish was also bleeding from his right sneaker. He had blown off his little toe on his right foot hunting ducks the week before he arrived in Bradenton. A few days after working out in Florida, his foot started to bleed again. Hunter pleaded with me: "Please don't tell Finley. He'll be pissed."

Fish was a power pitcher, and his fastball had late movement that made it tough to hit from either side of the plate. He pitched with precision and guile, moved the ball inside and out at will, and pitched quickly and without emotion. A decade later our paths would meet again after he underwent a contract dispute with Charlie Finley. Catfish would be granted free agency status and leave the A's and become the highest-paid pitcher in baseball when he signed with the Yankees in 1975—a move that catapulted Catfish's fortunes but was catastrophic to my future with the venerable old NY team. But more on that later.

While my roommate cemented his spot in the rotation in record time, the majority of my rookie year was spent spitting sunflower seeds while sitting on the bench. With youthful optimism before every game, I would go over to the lineup card to see if my name was included in the batting order. Day after day I had to deal with the fact that my name was again absent from the list. Much to my dismay I generally "rode the pines." Not at all what I had in mind. It's not that I didn't come to the ballpark ready and willing. On the contrary, I arrived early every day anxious to prove my value to the organization. My constant bench companion was Coach Luke Appling.

Lucius Benjamin Appling was a Hall of Fame shortstop who played his twenty-year career for the Chicago White Sox. Appling was legendary for two things: hitting and complaining about his ailments. His ailments were extensive.

He complained every day about minor aches and pains, a sore back, weak shoulders, shin splints, and his joints. As a result, he earned the name "Old Aches and Pains."

Appling was one of the great hitters in the American League with an uncanny ability to foul off pitches he didn't like. Rumor has it that he once fouled off twenty pitches in a row on purpose when ownership refused to give him some baseballs to autograph because they were too expensive; rumor has it he was never refused a ball again. One of Luke's favorite tricks was to foul balls into the opposing dugout. He would rifle foul balls in there, scattering coaches and players. At the age of fifty-seven, he was still able to hit fungos tirelessly during batting practice.

Like so many of the ballplayers of his era, Luke had true grit, the kind of hard-scrabbled, determined player emblematic of the tough Depression times. Luke had been through the War too. In his mind, every day he could put on a uniform was a good day and he imparted that enthusiasm to every person he encountered. When he didn't have a chew, Luke had a cigar.

I met Luke one day when he was sitting in a four-foot, one-hundred-degree aluminum whirlpool tub with a cigar in his mouth, spilling ashes in the water as he spoke. Holding court in the trainer's room, his lecture concerned his perception of truth: "If you want to have a long career, don't tell anyone the truth, especially yourself. If you want to make the press laugh, tell them what you think."

But Luke didn't just spout words of wisdom, and his actions on the field spoke for themselves. In fact, Luke claims credit for the longest at-bat in baseball history.

"In a game in the 1940 season, I fouled off twenty-four pitches in one trip to the plate." That was not an exaggeration. "Red Ruffing [Yankees] was pitching, and I decided to have some fun. So I started fouling off his pitches," Appling said. "I took a pitch every now and then, but after twenty-four fouls, old Red could hardly lift his arm, and I walked. That's when they took him out of the game, and he cussed me all the way to the dugout."

I became Luke's pet project, a season-long work in process. "We need to understand what's going on in your mind when you're at the plate," he said. "Then we need to focus on whatever it is that's going on in there. You know, weed out the bad stuff and put in the good." Luke leaned over to me and said, "You don't have to put every ball in play. Pitchers are going to try to get you to swing at their pitches. Piss on them. You need to see the ball in the zone where you want it and put that ball in play." Luke and I talked about how hard it was to be a part of the game "from a seat on the bench" and the challenges in keeping your thoughts focused on the game and staying ready, loose, and mentally "in" the game. I learned a lot about the game, how to play the game, and how to stay ready.

Finley bought controlling interest of the Athletics' franchise in 1960 and replaced Connie Mack's elephant with a Missouri mule—not just a cartoon logo, but a real mule, which he named after himself: Charlie O the Mule. Reportedly to make us all feel at home when we left Kansas City for parts unknown, Finley brought his mule, Charlie O, to join us at hotels across the country. I remember it "relieving itself" on the floor of the Hilton lobby while the press was interviewing Charlie about his newest signing of Rick Monday.

Charlie never tired of trying out little things that annoyed the visiting teams. Charlie was a ringmaster in charge of a circus. Caged monkeys cackled a welcome to the park, and sheep decked out in A's collars and straw hats grazed on the center field grass incline just beyond the fence. A mechanical rabbit named "Harvey" behind home plate offered the umpire new baseballs. "Little Blowhard," a compressed-air device inside of home plate, blew dirt away. Helium balloons with A's tickets soared throughout the city, and he even shot off fireworks in the park. Unfortunately, the neighbors complained and the city made him desist. Once, Miss USA served as batgirl. In 1964, Charlie even persuaded the Beatles to play in the ballpark.

Charlie's ideas were always inventive and rarely went off without some hitch. Farmers Day—one of a series of promotions that Finley used to draw people into the ballpark— was no exception to that mayhem. Other such promotions included Hot Pants Night and Satchel Paige Night. There would be a milking contest, a greased pig catching contest, a mule riding contest, and an egg hunt for the children.

The 1965 Farmers Day that summer had more than a few surprises for everyone involved but, as usual, there were several problems connected with this promotion. The problems started with the greased pig contest that went way past the allotted time. Catfish cautioned us in the clubhouse, "I grew up on a farm, and I can tell you that no matter what size that pig is, a greased pig cannot be easily wrestled to the ground." After countless futile attempts by individual participants, an army of fifteen men finally corralled the pigs. The pigs strutted off the field, emboldened in their victory.

Additional problems appeared with the promotion. The cows did not want to be milked in front of everyone, and the mule couldn't, or wouldn't, be ridden. Charlie offered one hundred dollars to any player who could ride his mule. "Hawk" Harrelson took him up on the offer and tried to ride the mule around the field, but it almost bucked him off. He was hanging on to it by the neck hairs trying to get John Wyatt to stop the thing. Diego Seguí was the only player I knew who could ride the stupid thing.

Charlie Finley himself asked the field manager, Mel McGaha, to call a meeting and stress how important this type of event was to the ballclub. Players hated any kind of pre-game meeting. This was their leisure time, but coach Charles Leo "Gabby" Hartnett, a six-time All Star and future Hall of Fame catcher with the Chicago Cubs, bellowed out over the clubhouse din, "Meeting in five minutes." Everyone grumbled, but gathered anyway, mostly undressed and uninterested. McGaha was not a motivational speaker. He said, "Everyone dressed and on the field for Farmers Day. No exceptions." Some players seemed more into it than others, and a mischievous grin washed over one of them.

Farmers Day offered a whole new level of off-the-wall options to the most fun-loving of ball players. In one particular case, a teammate decided to play a joke on the farmers and their families coming in to see the game and, not wanting to leave anyone out, he thought he might as well include the umpires and the grounds crew as well. As legendary rumor has it (which might or might not be totally factual), this player snuck in before batting practice and fed the monkeys amphetamines (greenies) by putting them inside grasshoppers and enticing the monkeys to eat the insects.

It should be noted that Major League Baseball did prohibit this type of amphetamines in 2006, but at this time, it was still very much a part of the locker room culture of the sport. Like hot dogs and beer, greenies were "widely available," according to former players like Mike Schmidt of the Philadelphia Phillies. The pills were in all clubhouses, often dispensed by team trainers and other medical personnel. "They were obtainable with a prescription," Schmidt writes, "but be under no illusion that the name on the bottle always coincided with the name of the player taking them before game time."

These pills energized players and helped some to get through a tough series of games among a grueling one-hundred sixty-two game schedule. It was important not to take a pill prematurely. Players liked to tell of teammates who took pills before games, then had the games rained out and spent the rest of the night climbing the walls. In my twelve-plus years in the big leagues, I never physically saw a player take one, but I did witness players on certain days who exhibited extraordinary behavior.

For the fans coming in to see Farmers Day in Kansas City, the monkeys were exhibiting strange behavior and their cage was becoming a formidable obstacle. The fans entered the upper concourse in left field and walked through the zoo area.

It was a beautiful summer evening—warm, but pleasant, with a slight chance of showers. No one expected to encounter raucous and rowdy chimps. The monkeys were still in their enclosure but just barely. Two were shaking their cages in unison so fiercely that it looked like the ten-foot-wide structure might give way. One was intent on squeezing through the bars. He spit at a little girl walking by holding her mother's hand. Then he urinated on a little boy. The public address announcer asked the zoo custodian to report to the right field zoo area as quickly as possible.

In addition to the monstrous monkey behavior, the sheep in center field were butting heads with one another and trying to jump on to the field. A few minutes later, the petting zoo was closed after one of the children was supposedly bitten by an enraged duck.

Charlie O, the mule, made an entrance coming down the right field line and experienced an extreme case of diarrhea all over first base. The crowd was trying to look away, while my teammate sat howling in the corner of the dugout with a towel over his head. The phone in the dugout rang. Finley was on the line.

"Where is he?" he demanded. The player in question came to the phone on the wall near the bat rack and the runway to the locker room.

"This is Charlie," he yelled. The player at the other end was holding the phone away from his head. "Did you give greenies to the mule?" he asked.

"No," he replied. "I gave them to the monkeys, the ducks, and the sheep."

"What did you give to the mule?"

"Chewing tobacco," he said, holding his sides.

"Did you give anyone else greenies?" demanded Finley. There was a pause on the other side of the phone. "I put a few in the grounds crew's drinking water," he said. Charlie could then be heard dialing the other phone for the head of the grounds crew.

The game started despite these irregularities and seemed to progress normally, except for an impromptu fistfight amongst the grounds crew perched in canvas alley. The night continued to be full of surprises. The second pitch in the second inning was fouled into the stands, and the home plate umpire requested more baseballs. Instead of a bat boy handing him more balls, the umpire pushed a button and a mechanical rabbit named "Harvey," with red eyes blinking, rose out of two trap doors in the ground right behind home plate with new baseballs for the umpire and, at the same time, blew dirt off home plate with a compressed-air device.

The problem was that, along with the baseballs in the rabbit hole, the grounds crew had hidden a dozen pigeons before batting practice. The pigeons had been cooped up for about two hours. The skit was designed to frighten the umpires, which it did. However, when the doors popped open on the new ball dispenser, fear was felt throughout the ballpark. The pigeons were released and began to fly. They circled the field, low and fast, defecating on players, farmers, and families for several minutes before they took roost up in the rafters under the right-field overhang. Clothing was ruined, food destroyed. After fifteen minutes of ducking, the crowd's attention was diverted back towards the field. The concessions quickly ran out of napkins.

About a month later, on September 25, I walked into the clubhouse and noticed that my nameplate had been moved over in its holder at the top of the locker and another one had been added. The two names were half in and half out and looked like they might fall at any moment. PAIGE was the other name. I wondered who this rookie was. I didn't recognize his name.

The A's locker room was right out of central casting, a quadrangle of old wooden coops with wooden stools arranged to give seniority to the players who had played the longest. Clothes were thrown all over. The colorful combinations of yellow, white, and green tops and bottoms made just getting dressed correctly a challenge.

I was the youngest player in the league, who had fallen victim to the oldest gremlin in sports—insecurity. I wasn't playing very often and, when I did get the opportunity, I wasn't playing well. My poor performance was keeping me out of the starting lineup and out of sight. So far it hadn't resulted in a pink slip, and so I was relieved to see that I at least still had half a locker. In addition to the normal wooden stool that usually stood in front of my locker, a rocking chair had been pushed in. It didn't fit the corner very well, crowding everything around it, but it did seem to fit the turn of the century motif in the old clubhouse.

INSIGHT PITCH

About an hour before game time, a string bean of a man sauntered in, headed in my direction. He was black with long gangly arms, a hat with a turned up front brim, a face that had seen some action over the years, and a whimsical sparkle in his eyes.

"Satchel," he said and held out a bony hand. Looks like Al Zeke, the clubhouse man, had put the youngest player in the league with the oldest.

Leroy "Satchel" Paige was a local legend. His reputation as one of the best pitchers in the Negro League was unsurpassed. As a child, he acquired the nickname "Satchel" when he worked as a porter at a railroad station. He honed his pitching skills in reform school. In his prime, despite his enormous baseball talent, Satchel was barred from playing in the major leagues for years because of his race. He started with Chattanooga in the Negro League and went on to record over one hundred wins, depending on who you asked. Because there were very few statistics kept by teams in those days, Satchel kept his own notebook of game results. Satchel was a crowd-pleaser. As the headliner attraction, he often pitched the first couple of innings, but not long enough to get the win or loss. The weather-beaten persona came from years of barnstorming in countless small towns across America against semi-pros, sand lotters, actually anyone with the money to pay to see a baseball icon. Lured by dollar signs, Satchel jumped from one team to another, breaking all kinds of records while attracting record-breaking crowds wherever he went. It's been noted that he pitched two or three games a week and, for most of his career, was virtually un-hittable. He even pitched both games of doubleheaders.

Perhaps to his annoyance, Satchel Paige was not the first black baseball player to get a shot in the major leagues. That honor would go to a warrior athlete called Jackie Robinson. Unlike Jackie's more stoic persona, Satchel's volatile personality would have undoubtedly produced problems with both players and fans. Paige was among the first handful of black baseball players accepted into the predominantly white major leagues. Dazzling fans with his dominating style into his forties and fifties, Paige believed that, "Age is a question of mind over matter. If you don't mind, it doesn't matter."

In a tribute to the Negro Leagues, and to contribute to the A's financial bottom line, Finley had hired Paige to pitch one last game in Kansas City, making him the oldest pitcher ever to throw in the major leagues at fifty-nine years, two months, and ten days.

Two minutes after arriving in the locker room, Satchel was holding court in the corner of the clubhouse.

"Satchel, are you going to pitch today?"

"Man, I'm not sure I can. I haven't been feelin' too well lately. I'm going to be sixty in a few weeks you know."

His performance was certainly not as sickly as his press conference might have suggested. At the age of fifty-nine, an arbitrary age since he could not produce a birth certificate, Paige pitched three scoreless innings of one-hit ball for the Kansas City Athletics. Satchel remains the oldest player to pitch in the major leagues. He only needed twenty-nine pitches to depose the players from the Boston Red Sox lineup that included Carl Yastrzemski. As was his habit in the Negro Leagues, he instructed his outfielders to sit down in the third inning because he planned on striking everyone out.

At the time that Paige arrived in the locker room, I was one of the youngest players in league history, having just turned nineteen in August. The differences between us were profound. On the one hand, there's a black man from a poor background, getting on in years, able to command enormous respect in a lily-white-man's game dominated by privilege and power, a game that discriminated against him exclusively because of his color but a game he still embraced with infectious enthusiasm. He had made peace with the negative demons and, on that day, was reveling in being the center of attention.

I myself, on the other hand, was perhaps the most ill-equipped person to ever put on such a green uniform. I came from an all-white working-class environment and a private all-boys' parochial high school in a conservative suburb. I had lost my youthful confidence as I struggled daily with deceptive curveball demons. I was pressing, trying to impress anyone and everyone. Spooked by constantly being in the spotlight, I definitely was not having any fun.

As I thought about the things Satchel said to me that day and, more importantly, about the way he said them, I came to realize the message he was really trying to impart. Although we only spent a brief time together, his ability to look at life from a different perspective stayed with me for a long time. Satchel had an impressive presence. He was not focused on the injustices of the past and not concerned about the future. He lived life for today. Somehow, he had perfected the ability to be present in the moment. Satchel, sitting next to me at the back of the locker room, said, "Don't take yourself too seriously. Be happy with what you have and keep moving forward with a smile on your face."

****

Navigating the transition from being center stage in private school suburban Boston baseball to playing understudy at third base in the big leagues for Kansas City was a bridge too far. Looking back, I was just too young and naive to react properly to the pressure and opportunities that were all around. I was certainly unable to overcome my decided lack of experience in pressure situations. So many games. Game after game, coming one after another, turned out to be an avalanche of negative plays, miscues, swings, and misses.

There was, to be sure, an "old boys" environment where many players from the South were not as welcoming to players from the North, but I think that I could have overcome that prejudice if I had been able to hit a little and field the way I knew I could. There have been very few players who came from high school and walked into pro baseball and never looked back. I was not destined to be counted in that number. One thing was very clear; I did not have a good vision of myself in uniform acting like I belonged there.

CHAPTER 11
1966 CHANGEUPS

BY THE END of the 1966 spring training season, baseball and I were not on the same wavelength. The Kansas City Athletics wanted to capture a pennant and management only wanted to suit up players who could successfully ride the tides. I had great hang ten potential but wipeout numbers. I was at an impasse, barely treading water, and was sent down to the minor leagues to work on my form. Only two years into my career, I felt like Marty McFly heading back from the future. In order to reach the success I wanted, I needed to control the present, by doing things more naturally, more gracefully. I told myself that my career was still on the rise, but realized that getting back to the big leagues was not going to be an easy ride. Deep down, I knew I still had a lot to learn.

Modesto, California, 1966

Assigned to the Modesto Reds, in the California league, I was a long way from home and even farther from the major leagues. Sharing the field with teammates Reggie Jackson, Rollie Fingers, and Tony LaRussa, all of whom would become members of the Baseball Hall of Fame, I was enjoying baseball again. Because I had received a substantial bonus, my spot in the lineup was secured in permanent ink. Playing on a regular basis, I was improving both my batting and fielding, and I even got a chance to pitch one shutout inning during a game where the entire pitching staff had been used up. In the early part of August, an inside fastball broke a bone in my left hand and issued me an early exit from the land of milk and honey. The team went on to win the California League Championship.

Fort Dix, New Jersey, 1967

In early January 1967, two important letters arrived in the mail at 222 Ridgewood Drive. One letter was the standard uniform contract from the Kansas City Athletics' front office. It was signed by my friend Pat Friday. He mistakenly misspelled my name again, this time calling me Charles. Perhaps this was an ongoing joke between us, but on closer inspection, with the salary basically the same as the year before, the offer was more of an outright insult than a welcome invitation to rejoin the Show.

The second letter contained even more of a shock and would have an even greater impact on my baseball career. It was from the United States Selective Service Agency, and it started off with the word "Greetings." I swallowed hard as I read the words. The tone was patronizing, but the reality was stark. I was being conscripted into military service, into the US Army and, in 1967, that meant I was shortly going to be involved in a shooting war in the jungles of Vietnam. This was the ultimate wake-up call.

At this point, I had no idea what was going to happen next in my life, never mind in my career. The letter went on to say that my induction physical was to be held at the Boston Armory on February 10 and that I should be prepared, should I pass, to take the oath of enlistment on the spot and also be ready to ship off to basic training immediately. I shivered.

On a damp, dreary, bone-chilling morning inside the Boston Army Headquarters, I stood and pledged to: "solemnly swear to support and defend the Constitution of the United States against all enemies, foreign and domestic" and "obey the orders of the President of the United States," as well as the orders of the Uniform Code of Military Justice.

An hour beforehand, I had been an athlete, a professional baseball player. I made my living hitting and fielding baseballs. Now I was going off to the field to be a soldier, attacking enemy lines. It didn't seem possible. But it was not only possible, it was happening very quickly.

I was stunned, trying to cope with all of the impossible scenarios. Because I signed a professional baseball contract directly out of high school, opting not to go to college, I did not have a 2S deferment—"Registrant deferred because of activity in study"—that was awarded my high school buddies, now slugging it out in freshman social science courses. If I had it, I would have been protected or at least deferred.

The fact that almost half of my bonus money was designated for assignment to the US Treasury made no difference in my eligibility status. I found myself on a bus on my way to Fort Dix, New Jersey—a winter address that would prove to be lots more than a vacation away from baseball. If I had to go, I felt fortunate to be entering the military as an army reservist, which was orchestrated by my state senator calling the Reserve Unit in Quincy and arranging for me to join ASAP. At least I wouldn't be heading to Vietnam directly after basic training, I hoped.

The bus arrived at the reception center at two in the morning, and fifteen minutes later, I was doing pushups in the snow beside the bus with Sergeant Walker barking insults directly in my ear. Fort Dix was the training facility for the war in Vietnam. It was twelve weeks of basic training followed by six weeks of advanced individual training, depending on your job.

Morning came in less than three hours. Tired and scared, we rolled out of the sack onto the glazed linoleum floor. We marched directly out of the barracks onto the field and stood at attention for an hour while the supply office opened slowly and were then handed an ill-fitting uniform, worse-fitting boots, and two funny-looking hats. Intermittently, we dropped and did more pushups, idled for hours in chilling rain while regimental committees conducted formal training, then marched back to the barracks again.

Learning to march in unison took a while. Learning to salute was also time-consuming, but the most challenging skill we had to master was taking orders without question. Properly maintaining the barracks was an exacting chore. A tall man with a Smokey the Bear hat on said, "Okay, men, give me your undivided attention." This is how most meetings would start, followed by instruction about: how you mop a floor, swab a latrine, make a bunk, stow belongings, police the area, scrub webbing, burnish brass, blouse trousers, spit shine shoes, fall in and fall out, stay in step, field strip rifles, perform the manual of arms, roll horseshoe packs, inflate air mattresses, puncture blisters, sterilize water, clean mess kits, stand inspection, and stand guard.

I slept in an eight-man bunk room. Our company got along pretty well, aside from a few fights about noise and room responsibilities. All in all, basic training unfolded as expected. I tried to stay out of the way . . . away from being noticed. One thing I did like about the military was there was a direct correlation between effort and results. The harder you tried, the more you succeeded.

Digging deep into my minimal survival skills, I was able to endure the long-forced marches with all the gear on. Physically, I was in excellent shape. The challenges I faced were more psychological. My first case of claustrophobia set in clambering through the sarin gas chamber, especially since one of the soldiers in my group dropped his gas mask as we unmasked in the chamber. That meant the entire squad had to go through again, more deliberately.

As much as I reveled in the camaraderie of my platoon, I was awfully relieved when basic training was over. I was the lone soldier separated from my troop, who was headed out to the Hanoi Hilton and assigned to AIT at a reserve unit near Hanover, Massachusetts. I definitely wasn't cut out to be a warrior soldier, but the experience brought me closer to an attitude of being much more purposeful and focused when I needed to be. Lessons learned to be applied to the game of baseball—a game I had acquired a whole new appreciation for from the perspective of the basic training field and sorely missed.

Burlington, Iowa

When I returned from the barracks to the ballfield, I felt like a rookie all over again. Timing is everything in baseball, and I discovered that my timing, both on and off the field, was way off. While I was off marching in the trenches, Sal Bando had marched in and entrenched himself firmly as the Athletics' everyday third baseman.

It was my fourth year in professional baseball, and I was back in A Ball in Burlington, Iowa. This was definitely not the script I had envisioned for my career. I knew that unless something changed soon the baseball chapter of my life would be over. While I was out of commission, my starring role was snagged by my understudy, and I couldn't help but wonder when, and if, another part might be available. Baseball is a great game, but it's also a business. Owners expect a return on their investment.

After striking out embarrassingly on a slow curveball that I thought was going to hit me the night before, I wasn't sleeping that well to begin with when I was rudely awakened by the phone in my hotel room. Charlie Finley was on the line. There was only one reason for him to be on the phone. I was going to be released. I waited for words like "not worth the money" and "sorry I had signed you in the first place." However, the tone of his voice fooled me, surrounding me with compassion.

"Skip," he said, more fatherly than I expected. "It's been a long time since we spoke last. How's it going?" We both knew how things were going. I told him the truth. After all, I owed him that. I said, "I am having trouble hitting, especially the curve, and the problems have compounded themselves to a point where it's affecting my attitude and confidence." We were both silent for a while. He said, "I'm getting reports that you might not be seeing the ball well and you're having trouble picking up the pitches." He was correct on both counts.

I pulled the phone away from my ear. Listening to the moment of silence, it felt like an eternity as I waited for the ax to fall. "I talked it over with the manager and the coaching staff, and we agree that some changes are needed," he said in a terminal tone of voice. I could not breathe.

"Skip," he said with enough impact that, had I been in the batter's box, I would have started my defensive moves to duck away. "We're interested in your thoughts . . . about becoming a pitcher, rather than an infielder. We all believe it would be in your best interest to capitalize on your God-given abilities and get away from some of the problems you're experiencing at the plate. We know how hard you have worked these last couple of years, but we think it's time to face the facts. You don't have a future in the organization as a hitter."

I stared down at the phone as if it were alive. This conversation was changing my life. But it wasn't ending it. Certainly, I had thought about pitching before. Every position player thinks about pitching. I never really took myself seriously, though, as a pitcher.

I flashed back to my childhood—holding the bat in the basement, looking in the mirror, picturing myself as a big leaguer—a batsman leading his team to championships. Getting lucrative endorsements. Driving fancy cars.

My life was leaking through the pores of this phone. In Charlie's voice, I heard a tone of separation. He was making a business deal, punctuated with a tincture of unexpected pity. I was numb. For a long perplexing moment, I hesitated, doubting myself. The sensation passed, and I raised the phone like a barbell and gripped hard onto the receiver.

"Charlie," I said. "I agree. For me, it's been a long and frustrating climb, and I hate where I am right now in my career. If you believe that I can help your ball club in any way, I'm all in. I will start the process of becoming . . . " I wait a bit for my heart to start up again, " . . . a pitcher as soon as possible."

"Perfect," he replied, not skipping a beat. "Smart," he added. "Here's the plan." Charlie said he was going to continue to pay me, but he wanted me to get some special pitching coaching from Bill Posedel, the minor league pitching coach, as soon as possible. He was sending me to the Athletics' spring training location for a one-on-one crash course on the mechanics of pitching. He closed with, "I'll send you instructions tomorrow . . . Good luck."

INSIGHT PITCH

The phone went silent. I felt dead. All those hours standing in front of the mirror as a child, all those years piecing together a dream to be the next Willie Mays, gone in a two-minute conversation. My batting career, my professional career reduced to a dial tone. I took a long pull on the air in the hotel room. Here I stood, changed completely by the mere mention of a word. I was now and forever more would be a pitcher. I shuddered to think what that meant.

CHAPTER 12
PITCHING IN

Houston Astros, 1968

LIKE MOST TRANSITIONS in sport, converting from the infield grass to the pitching rubber had its fair share of challenges. After receiving excellent one-on-one intensive instruction at the A's training facility in Arizona over the fall, I was very surprised to be sold on a "Look/See" basis to the Astros the following spring. Truth be told I did not really know for what position I had been purchased. Assuming I was still an infielder, I ran out to take grounders by third base on the first day of spring training only to be ordered—not too politely, I might add—to get in the outfield with the other pitchers.

I guess the Astros were not all that impressed with my crash course in the basic mechanics of pitching because I was sent back to Kansas City at the end of the spring. Not quite an auspicious start to inserting myself into the Athletics' starting rotation. Having missed another spring training in the

Athletics organization, I was unceremoniously assigned to A Ball to hone in on my pitching technique. By the end of the summer, I was encouraged to have progressed up the minor league ladder to AA and was hopeful for my prospects in 1969. And then, to my great surprise, I was acquired by the Seattle Pilots as a pitcher in the expansion draft. At least this time I was certain about the position.

Seattle Pilots/Milwaukee Brewers, 1969-1970

Six days after Major League Baseball approved the sale of the Seattle Pilots to Bud Selig and a consortium of Milwaukee businessmen, the Milwaukee Brewers opened up the 1970 season at Milwaukee's County Stadium. The city of Milwaukee was thrilled to have Major League Baseball back, but it was not so thrilled with the fact that the Brewers were part of the American League. Lacking the draw of recognizable National League star power, the Brewers found themselves also lacking sizable crowds in the stands. The organization had little time to initiate the hometown crowd to the new league and a new crop of unknown ballplayers. The Brewers struggled to fill the seats, a problem that would persist for almost a decade.

In an effort to rejuvenate local enthusiasm for the sport and jump-start its franchise, the front office scheduled an exhibition game against the Braves. The Braves roster was very familiar to the fans of Milwaukee. It would be good for business to host the Braves back in County Stadium, even if it wouldn't count in the record books. And so, on an off day early in the season, the newly minted Milwaukee Brewers hosted an exhibition game against the Atlanta Braves, a team of All-Stars led by Hank Aaron, Orlando Cepeda, and Clete Boyer. Both upper management and the loyal baseball fans of Milwaukee were excited about the contest, but the players were not so thrilled. Opposing teams had rolled over five straight wins, and the staff was exhausted; the last thing anyone in the bullpen wanted was to face a hot team from the other league. It didn't help that the pitching staff had started out poorly and was sinking harder than many of the starters' curveballs.

Dave Bristol, the Brewers' field manager, had no interest in wasting one of his struggling starters in such an exhibition. So the call went out to Portland, Oregon, home of the Brewers AAA team. When I arrived at the ballpark I was handed a round-trip ticket to Milwaukee for a one-day vacation to pitch to the opposing league's Hall of Fame superstars. I was thrilled to be going back to the bigs, even if it was only for a day.

Pitching an exhibition game is not usually a career-changing opportunity. However, in the early goings of the Milwaukee Brewers' season in 1970 inside the confines of County Stadium, a career-changing opportunity was exactly what it became.

The Atlanta Braves were riding a winning streak. The loyal Braves fans longed to see their heroes again and have one last glimpse of several Hall of Famers and, in particular, a guy named "Hammerin Hank," who was making history with every swing of the bat. The headlines in the *Milwaukee Sentinel* read, "Hank Aaron and Orlando Cepeda come back to honor Milwaukee and baseball fans everywhere." Safe to say I had an unparalleled chance to make a major statement.

Successfully shutting down the star-studded lineup, I pitched a complete game against the Atlanta Braves. I even had an exciting moment at the plate, guessing correctly when a tall lefty threw me a fastball, leading to my first home run. Impressed with my performance, the team opted not to ship me back to the minor leagues. Instead, I brought my "not quite ready for prime time" repertoire of pitches to the mound every five days, resulting in some pretty erratic pitching, marked every now and again with shocking brilliance. In my defense, our fielding was often unpredictable. One night the right fielder caught an easy fly ball and, tripping into the wall, tossed it over the fence by mistake. On another afternoon, one of my infielders ran to the mound and asked if I could please try to keep the ball away from him—he had a miserable hangover and was having trouble bending down to field a grounder. All in all, it was a very stressful and confusing time for me.

Dave Bristol was the tobacco-chewing, blunt-spoken manager. His country charm and farm wisdom was somewhat lost on the team that was made up basically of off-the-wall players that the other teams didn't protect in the recent expansion draft, many of whom were infamously featured in Jim Bouton's book *Ball Four*.

On one particular Sunday afternoon in July, I got the opportunity to get to know Bristol even better than before. I was starting against the Detroit Tigers on a glorious midsummer afternoon that showcased gleaming sunshine and light breezes off Lake Michigan. I was struggling to regain my focus that day, after another routine double-play ball went through the shortstop's legs. Frustrated to a fault, I was trying to throw the ball too hard. My fastball was straight. My curveball was straighter. With the score three to zero in favor of the Tigers, I walked the first two batters to start the fourth inning.

The Milwaukee game-day announcer, Bob Uecker, was relating a story about a fishing trip he had just taken to the Upper Peninsula—anything to take the viewers' minds off the play on the field. Uecker paused his tall tale and opined, "You know, it's nice to see the manager going out to say something encouraging to his young pitcher. It's a good strategy to build up his confidence and settle him down."

Ten feet toward the third-base side rubbing up a new, and hopefully better behaved, baseball, I looked over and saw Bristol standing on the mound. I suppose I should have been standing there waiting for him. I climbed back up the little hill, trying to avoid his eyes, and reached out my hand to give him the baseball. He spoke up in a calm, almost sedated, tone. "Ain't no one warming up, so don't try to give that there baseball to me. I ain't gonna pitch. You are." He seemed to be collecting his thoughts. I could smell the tobacco on his breath. Only inches away now as he spat fragments of Beechnut loose leaf onto my face, he made it clear that my duty was to get out of the inning unscathed, or I might be heading back to the minors. By the end of the discussion, his voice was quivering with rage. Then he turned toward the dugout and trotted back to his spot at the end of the bench.

We won the game five to three. I recorded the victory with a complete game performance. As the reporters gathered around to chat me up after the great and unexpected turnaround pitching effort, I was seething white with anger. I spoke to no one and pushed past them on my way across the locker room to Bristol's office. I went it and slammed the door. He was changing his clothes. He turned around and said, "You're mad and you want to fight me. Good! If you pitch every game the way you did the last few innings, we can have a fight every time, if you want, until you grow up. Now get out of here and leave the door open."

That winter Dave Bristol sent me a three-page handwritten letter. Much of the territory had already been covered, but he wanted to say how proud he was that I was able to stand up to the pressures of pitching in Milwaukee and how proud he was to have me on his team.

Mayagüez, Puerto Rico, 1970

Cal Ermer, the Milwaukee bench coach, came to me toward the end of the season and asked me to play winter ball for the Mayagüez Indios, a team he was going to manage in Puerto Rico. He told me that the pay was bad but the island was beautiful. Of course, I accepted the invitation, fully aware that refusing would virtually kill any chance I had of starting with the Brewers again next season. Having traded in my third baseman's mitt for a pitching glove two years before, I had just completed my first full year of pitching. With exceptionally frustrating backup, I had compiled an extraordinarily poor statistical season with the cellar-dwelling Milwaukee Brewers. A member of the press corps reported that I must have some extraordinary raw talent because, with that kind of a record, any other ball club would have released me before the All-Star break.

My wife and I had married during the season and spent our "honeymoon" on a romantic road trip to Detroit and Cleveland. Needless to say, we were both looking forward to a lovely tropical getaway. Arrangements were made for us to stay at La Palma Hotel in the middle of old Mayagüez. The economy of Mayagüez was centered around tuna packing, not tourism. La Palma was not listed in the top six places to stay on the island, but it was where all six of the American ballplayers would reside. Our apartment consisted of a bed and a chair, a circa 1950 vintage kitchen set straight out of *The Honeymooners*, an extremely uncomfortable mattress we had to drag to the floor, and a small sink and mini fridge where the cockroaches congregated. When we first moved in, we were surprised by how much company the apartment next door seemed to entertain, even late into the evenings. Weeks later our suspicions were confirmed that the voluptuous vixen next door catered to a pay-by-the-hour clientele.

Larger-than-life teammate Bill Lee joined us at La Palma. He was pitching enthusiastically, but erratically, for the Red Sox and was sent to winter ball to work on his control. Bill, his wife, and their newborn baby lived above us. Between the constant commotion in the adjoining apartment and the noise of the infant upstairs, the quiet serenity of our island retreat was laughable.

Bill was a fastballing left-hander, a showman with a flair for the dramatics who was never short of opinions. He was an ideal teammate. Bill, however, took exception to some of the showboat antics of the local ballplayers, many of them known to be hot dogs. One player who, in Bill's mind, was particularly egregious was local favorite Elrod Rodriguez. Ellie took too long getting into the batter's box for Bill's taste. His routine included scratching out the back line of the box as he took a half dozen practice swings. Bill looked in from the mound at all these shenanigans and grew increasingly impatient. When Ellie finally took his stance in the box, the first pitch hit him in the ribs. While not totally intentional, it appeared to be a message pitch. Ellie Rodriguez took it personally, and the incident started a maelstrom.

Ellie didn't like being plunked by this winter ball pitcher vacationing in his native country. So he did what any former golden gloves champion would do—he charged the mound to have a few words with Bill about the proper conduct for guests in his native island. Bill looked away deliberately, waiting for Ellie to get out to the mound. Upon his arrival, Bill shed his non-pulsed, not-really-interested demeanor and raising his left arm, sucker-punched Ellie, lifting him off his feet and onto the ground. Ellie was down, and the fight was over. The incident left Ellie seething. He vowed to get even. The local papers got wind of the story and added to the sensationalism of the encounter by writing about it with inflammatory language, fueling the bad feelings between the towns of Mayagüez and Caguas.

A week later the Mayagüez bus pulled up to the Caguas ballpark for a night game. The crowd outside the bus was out for blood, and a confrontation ensued. Pete Koegel, a 6-foot-6 outfielder with head-to-foot muscles, led the Mayagüez team off the bus and tried to protect Bill while he exited the bus. Even with the rest of the team huddled around Bill, Pete could not protect him. Bill got pushed from behind, lost his balance, and fell forward onto the curb. More than Bill's pride was hurt, though. He landed flat on his face, wrenching his shoulder and losing a couple of teeth in the front of his mouth. His stint in winter ball was over. Bill and his teeth were on their way back to New England for repairs.

Little did I know that my learning experience in Puerto Rico was about to change my life. The life changer appeared as a simple, slightly stooped man in his mid-forties, sporting a short ponytail and worn-out sneakers. He would never be mistaken for a player, even though he was on the field for every game. And although he would never hit a home run or fire a fastball for strike three, he had amazing talents. Both on and off the field his gentle influence and curious way of framing things for me would impact my life for years to come.

Nelson Decker was the Indios' trainer, and I met him my first day in Mayagüez. Ordinarily, the team trainer was just a person who could rub out a sore shoulder or wrap an ankle. Nelson had a lot more to offer and, because of the long bus rides the Indios team took to play other teams on the island, I got to know him better than most.

Located at the far western end of the island, the Indios faced some prodigiously long bus rides through some of the most beautiful and rugged roads that were goat trails in another life. As the vintage bus slogged through mountain passes and past sheep, horses, and pigs in the road, there was a lot of time to think. One day, stuck behind some local goat herding traffic, Nelson began to tell me about a shaman he knew and worked with in Brazil, sharing bizarre accounts of surgeries that were being performed on people without medical instruments and without any anesthesia. The stories were wild and visceral with images of a patient lying on a fly-infested operating room with a blood-spattered, smock-clad doctor reaching inside, using their hands to pull out a tumor in his stomach and ruptured appendix. In response to my dismissing rolled eyes, Nelson said that he himself didn't believe the stories at first, but when he assisted in some of these operations, he began to understand the power of spirits that were beyond our culture and part of another world. Nelson wasn't intent on convincing me of the veracity of these feats, but he was insistent that I should at least open my mind to things that I didn't understand at first glance.

As the bus rides continued during the winter ball season, I would sit next to Nelson, intrigued by his tales. He was a very interesting man. While I am not totally certain about many of his claims, his strange ability to have premonitions leading to specific advice he shared with me left me pretty convinced that he was clairvoyant. He certainly was much more gifted than your average sports trainer. He was insightful, thoughtful, and convinced of the importance of the mind/body connection.

One thing we discussed on many of our long bus rides was my substantial vision issues. My glasses prescription was -450, making me legally blind without them on. Unfortunately, Uncle Sam seemed to have no problem with my lack of visual acuity. Nelson listened to me as I complained and understood my frustration of having to constantly deal with sweating, steamy, and cosmetically unattractive glasses. Nelson said I should consider the eyes to be "muscles" that should respond to positive exercise just like any other part of the body.

He told me that he had helped numerous people strengthen their eyes and improve their vision. The day after the conversation, a Tibetan eye chart lay folded on the wooden stool in front of my locker. I picked it up and turned it over a couple of times. It looked like a large snowflake crudely drawn on a white piece of paper. I headed for the trainer's room for an explanation. Rubbing the soreness out of yesterday's pitcher, Nelson began talking in his signature low, rhythmic tone. He explained to me how for generations the people of Tibet have used natural methods to correct visual weakness and improve their eyesight. Chief among them was a figure designed by Tibetan Lama Monks to give the necessary corrective exercises and stimulation to the muscles and nerves of the optical system. Nelson explained that the snowflake chart had a spot in the middle for my nose. The eye muscles must focus in and out, similar to a camera shutter. The purpose of these exercises was to strengthen the eye muscles to improve vision. Nelson suggested that I start out using it twice a day.

So I said I would try it and see—so to speak. I began with a few minutes' practice, morning and evening. With the palm of each hand, I'd first cup both closed eyes to relax them. Then I'd move the eyes clockwise around the outer circle of dots, repeating this movement in a counterclockwise rotation. Next, I moved the eyes back and forth between the dots at two and eight o'clock and repeated the movement between dots at four and ten o'clock. Then, with the palm of each hand in a cup shape, I closed my eyes to relax them again. Nelson suggested that I move the eyes clockwise on the outer edge of each of the arms and repeat the movement in a counterclockwise rotation. Having struggled with poor eyesight for most of my life, I admit that I was pretty skeptical when I started these exercises but, whether it was the exercises, the local tequila, or the tropical humidity, my vision improved dramatically for the duration of that winter season.

Unfortunately, my time on the beautiful island of Puerto Rico was cut short. Up to my old tricks trying too hard and throwing awkwardly, I developed some inflammation in my right arm and was sent home early. The clock seemed to be ticking on my career.

Through my conversations with Nelson, I discovered I could control things that I thought were out of my control by focusing my mind and picturing what I wanted my future to be. Mental imagery paved the way for my future success. Picturing and imagining became a discipline and a language for me. The very word "image" suggests a picture and a thought process, which in turn gave me power to control the outcome of events in the future, being able to envision what I was going to do, exactly what that looked like, sounded like, and smelled like and how I was going to feel.

Later in my life after baseball, I was able to study these elements academically. I received training in sports mental imagery from Columbia University in a doctoral program called the Psychosocial Studies of Human Movement and pursued an advanced degree in Sports Psychology. During my training, I was able to work with many athletes. Most were amateurs using mental imagery as a tool. With them, I always emphasized that what they allowed themselves to think would have a profound impact on their performances.

My studies included using the imagery as a rehearsal tool. For me, making the rehearsal as clear and personal as I could made all the difference. First, I wanted to picture myself on the mound, as if I were watching a movie of myself. I tried to stay completely positive. If I encountered mistakes or pictures of poor performance crept in, I would block them and immediately go to rewind. Next, I would bring the camera inside and see the game with my own eyes. I would concentrate and focus on my feelings about what I was seeing. As much as I could, I would involve sights, sounds, physical sensations, thoughts, and emotions. Seeing things clearly can help a person overcome nervousness. Feeling good about what's coming is a habit that comes from good planning. It's a real and very powerful sensation. Finally, I had to find the time to do it. Again, practice makes perfect, and eventually, I could engage the imagery process in little bite-size sessions, slow motion, frame by frame.

INSIGHT PITCH

At Columbia, I studied these techniques as they were first introduced by Richard Bandler and John Grinder as a cure for phobias in 1979. Golfer Jack Nicklaus has also said he's used mental imagery for every shot. The technique has significant anecdotal and clinical support, including its applications far beyond sports.

When I pitched for the Mets, I would find a quiet place to elevate my feet with my spikes on and mentally watch myself pitch in the upcoming game. At first, the visual imagery was from a distance, as though I was part of the crowd watching from the grandstand. Next, I would focus on myself, a one-frame-at-a-time motion picture. I would refine the images so I could watch my landing leg and my follow-through. It would gradually heighten my awareness. I would relax any tension and breathe methodically, trying to reach a deeper and deeper state of relaxation, bringing the pictures more and more into focus.

Next, I would get "in the zone." I'd go inside my own eyes and capture a recent pitch by pitch performance. I'd see the ball leave my hand, see it finish into the catcher's mitt, and hear my foot hit the dirt on my follow-through. I would hear the crowd roar. I would try to include as much realism as I could—vividness was a key. I would do this activity three times before the game and sometimes in between innings.

The two big takeaways for me was a physical relaxation and a sense that I could handle any situation that came my way. It really didn't take too much time, but if my mind wandered, I would bring it back. I'd reinforce it with scripts that I could play back to myself on the field and list it in a journal book that I maintained on the hitters.

Noted Brookline, Massachusetts, sports psychologist and former colleague Dr. Harvey Dulberg claims that many amateur athletes cannot distinguish between actual physical movement and one that is vividly imagined. Practice occurs when the athlete actually performs the action as well as when the athlete vividly imagines performing the action because similar neural pathways to the muscles fire in either case. These practices have become more mainstream over the years.

CHAPTER 13

STRIKE ONE . . .
PLAYERS' STRIKE, 1972

THE MAJOR LEAGUE Baseball basic contract is a currency tool, an exchange of value. It exists as a uniform document of understanding and agreement between services provided and men able to contract for them. The contract is not to blame for shortened careers, missteps, and generations of regrets left behind. It is not to blame for players being dealt with in shallow, callous, indifferent ways. The contract is not useful in the purchase of happiness; it will not give players a code of values, will not provide them with a purpose, and will not buy intelligence for a fool, better career stats for a slacker, or admiration for a coward.

Once a drafted player picked up a pen and signed on the bottom line with an organization, his ability to freely barter his playing services was erased before the ink was dry on the document. Through rigorous workouts and conscientious conditioning, a professional player could control his talent, but he had very little control over the path of his individual career, steering away from dangers and toward potentials.

Before the changes rendered in the 1970s and early '80s, the professional baseball contract was basically a chattel agreement that stipulated the terms of individual contracts. The contract covered the circumstances in which the owner was allowed to control the property he owned, in this case the players. The resulting contract continued to be an indenture. A lifetime agreement with two spaces for changes: the name and amount. Everything else was pretty much etched in stone.

A player's career was acutely managed by club owners and general managers. Year after year, the player entered into his contract negotiation with eyes wide open, sometimes willingly, more often reluctantly, devoid of any other option. A player under contract with a major league team had two options: play or go home. If you signed the contract, you were welcome to enter the clubhouse, but if you refused to sign, the door was permanently closed behind your back. The route home was full of many slippery side streets. Playing offered its own share of precarious pathways. A player could be traded or sold, waived, released, or assigned to the minor leagues with or without his knowledge or consent. The old salts, grizzled veterans of parks in all the professional leagues, would tell you, "That was the way it was." Generations of players just signed the submission without any alternative.

Compensation has always been part of scorekeeping in baseball. It separates the winners from the losers. The collective bargaining agreement (CBA) is the negotiated agreement that outlines the most up-to-date tenants. Baseball is distinctive in that collective bargaining does not directly set wages for employees. Instead, baseball salaries are determined by individual negotiations between a player (usually represented in today's mega-money market by an agent) and his team. But the collective bargaining agreement creates benefits such as salary arbitration and free agency, which greatly influences the outcomes of individual negotiations.

My career spanned parts of three decades: the '60s, the '70s, and the '80s. Significant changes were made to baseball's basic agreement during that period which mirrored the social changes that erupted in society at that time. "Let freedom ring," was a call to action that emanated across the nation in the sixties. MLB was finally fielding an integrated team on the field, but off the field the "reserve clause" restricted the freedom of all players. Players were owned outright by the team owners and even devalued on their personal tax returns. With the advent of televised games, the revenue flowing into MLB teams skyrocketed. The players received little benefit from this influx of funds. The Players Association argued that the players should share in this newfound wealth but did little to force the issue.

That all changed in 1966 when the Players Association hired veteran United Steelworkers organizer Marvin Miller. Miller, the Players Union's new boss, was a centerpiece of the maelstrom. He immediately abandoned the previous patronizing posture, enforcing a more traditional trade union approach, confronting the owners with demands and backing them up with power.

Miller's big breakthrough came on the issue of free agency. Since the late nineteenth century, a reserve clause in players' contracts stipulated that the club to which a player belonged controlled the rights to that player, unless he was sold, traded, or released. In what economists call a "monopsony," there was only one buyer of a player's services. This arrangement kept players' salaries low.

Fitting into a major league uniform required wedging into a major league contract. In 1972, it was one size fits all. Mine was a little small. Major league contract language was basically a bombastic boilerplate, a product of years of wrangling between the league and the MLB Players Association. Every word and phrase pre-negotiated and lawyered within an inch of its life and sandwiched into an unreadable tomb tightly printed on three pages, single-spaced. It is my ardent belief that no one in the history of baseball has ever actually read the entire thing. I also believe that embedded somewhere in the text, is the word "yougottabeshittingme," just to see if anyone actually read it, but to date that has not been detected. The Uniform Contract had two empty spaces on the first page, one for the name of the club and one for the name of the player—both usually hand-printed in ink. My basic contract looked the same as Babe Ruth's and Joe DiMaggio's, with the exception of a couple of missing zeros.

Contract negotiation was an integral part of the game that no player liked. It required skills that were in no way connected to the "all for the good of the team" concept of baseball and hard-core psychological bullying that was not at all conducive to optimal on-field performance. In a minute, I was going to find out that salary negotiation was a contact sport in the cornfields of Wisconsin.

Before free agency, player agents were virtually unheard of. Players had very few options. You either signed the one-year contract you were offered, or you resigned from the game. Like the majority of players in the '60s and '70s, I did my own salary negotiations and, in doing so, I've been told, I had a fool for a client. I suppose it was part of the bravado of being a player and all. Who was better to be able to explain how and why I played? Who was better to represent how I would fit into the club in the future? Looking back, I was probably the worst person to handle the negotiations because I wanted to play so badly. In the final analysis, I would have paid them to wear the uniform.

In early January 1972, a week after my new contract arrived by regular mail, I called the front office and asked for a meeting with Frank "Trader" Lane, the general manager of the Milwaukee Brewers, "to talk things over." Talking things over was going to be quite a challenge because Frank Lane was four times my age and mostly deaf. Frank did all of the salary negotiation.

My salary in 1970 was the minimum, $12,000. My salary in 1971 was raised to $12,750, a concession to the league-wide rise in minimum salary. After posting a 10-15 record with no run support, a 3.33 ERA, and back-to-back one-hitters, the offer on the table this year again was set at the league minimum $13,500.

I walked into the reception area to discover that the receptionist was away at lunch. I scanned the room for a place to sit. There was a couch and two chairs at one end of the ten by ten room, looking like they were salvaged from a railroad station, all polished wood, paneling floor to ceiling, with the strong smell of wood cleaner, tobacco, and tuna salad. Mr. Lane's room stood fifteen feet away. The door was closed. The room I was sitting in was dark, suggesting that the Brewers were trying to save money not only on players' salaries but also on light bulbs. I looked over and saw a stack of old newspapers piled unevenly on the side chair, folded to the sports section with magic marker notations all over them. Behind the door, I could hear Frank having a heated telephone argument with another player who apparently just received his 1972 contract too.

"Yea, yea," he said bombastically. "I get that from everyone. You hit twenty points less than you did last year. You didn't get on base as much, and you struck out fifteen times more. The bat boy was on base more than you were. What do you think that kind of performance is worth these days?" he asked.

The player on the other end was screaming. I recognized the voice and the sound of desperation. I tried to shrink into the unyielding vinyl sofa cushions. The phone call remained one-sided for another three or four minutes. Finally, Frank picked up the phone, and mumbled "Sure . . . sure," trying to end the call. He was bored and hungry. Finally, he yelled, "Suit yourself," and hung up the receiver by slamming it on the cradle like a gavel.

There was a short period of silence on the other side of the wall, and then I heard an audible but significant expulsion of air. A few seconds later he opened the door and without looking at me said, "Come on in, Charlie."

I started in, but not being asked to sit, I stood as he wedged his oversized pinstriped suit, all three buttons straining, into the well-worn tufted leather chair behind what looked to be months of unread newspapers, office memos, and private documents. He opened the meeting gruffly.

"I thought we sent you a contract?" he said and waved at one of the seats in front of his desk for me to be seated. I sat down but didn't dare lean back. "And apparently for some reason, you haven't signed it yet," he continued, covering his mouth with a snort of indignation. He sat back smugly as the chair complained. I pushed my chair back too, but it bucked, stuck in the worn grooves in the rug. It banged up and down and stuck to its original position. He glared at me challengingly. "So I really don't know why you asked for this meeting since technically you're not on the team for next year at this point in time." He stopped in what appeared to be a well-practiced stony voice and rephrased for emphasis, "NOT a part of our team for next year . . . yet."

"I got the contract you sent to me, and I'm not going to sign it," I said, proud of myself for getting it out there. There was a weighty silence in the room. I knew he could hear my heart beating.

"Listen . . . son. Listen to what I have to say. That contract is a very fair offer. I thought the whole thing over . . . carefully thought it over, you understand, and compared it to everyone on the team with as poor a record as yours. All this before I sent it to you. Pure and simple. No one gets an optional raise this year. Not me. Not you. Not anyone. This team lost money last year, and you had a front row seat to every single one of those rotten games. We didn't score runs. We didn't hit with runners on base. We didn't play well at home. We played like shit on the road. We couldn't contain the opposition's offense. And we didn't draw many more than a handful of these Midwest farmers, who were probably trying to find the fairgrounds, to see the games." He paused again, appreciating the consternation building in his speech.

"To put it bluntly, we were awful as a team last year, top to bottom. You included. What I should do is get rid of each and every one of you and start all over," he said as a faraway and slightly glazed look washed his face. He rubbed his belly and blew a vapor of smoke towards the poorly lit table lamp ten feet away. "You know, that's not a bad idea," he mused, entertaining himself. "I'm going to send a memo tomorrow that states that any player who hasn't signed the contract by the end of the month should start looking for another job." He smiled at himself at the absurdity of the statement.

"I'm a baseball player. I pitched as well as I could for this team. We never scored any runs when I pitched. If I was with another team, my record would be much better. I need money to live," I said to him. "You're not paying me enough money to get an apartment or to pay for even a secondhand car." I could hear my voice beginning to grow hollow and whiney.

"Money is the root of all evil," he said to me, looking up for the first time, beginning to sermonize. "There's a lot of people living around here with a lot more talent than you demonstrated last year, who *are* willing to play for this team and probably for *less* money than I am paying you. You get paid to perform," he said. "It's simple—if you don't perform, you don't get paid. I'll probably get criticized by the higher-ups and the press just for putting you back in a uniform for next year and giving you another chance to put us in last place." He was talking now for his own benefit. There was a long pause.

"Are you a church-going fella?" he asked out of the blue. I nodded, but didn't say anything. "Do you read the Bible by any chance?" I nodded again. "Good. Good for you. I do too, not necessarily on a regular basis, you understand.

"Do you recall the fable about the money changers in the temple?" he asked. "I use the word 'fable' without any disrespect to any theological point of view, but because I wasn't actually there myself, I can't testify to the exact truth of the event." He sat back on the ornate chair, getting more and more pleased with the point he was making. His seat groaned as the wheels strained on the plastic rug protector. Clearly, this was not the first time he had told this story, maybe not even the first time that day.

"It seemed this fellow Judas was desperate for money. He did the most despicable thing by handing over his boss to demonic people who eventually did very bad things to him. Seems people will turn on their own family for the sake of money," he said. The story seemed to hit very close to home for him. "Did you remember ever reading about him any-where?" he asked mockingly.

We were way off track with my salary negotiations, and I didn't have any choice but to go along. My mind began to wan-der. I wondered if I was really negotiating my way to a civilian job as a bank teller. He finished, and an awkward silence again took over the room. He looked at me for a response. I looked back, vacantly, not able to remember what he just said and if he needed a question answered or if he had just stopped again for emphasis. We sat, staring at his pictures on the wall, a team photo from the Braves 1960 season, an autographed bat. Ten seconds went by slowly.

He said, "I do remember a couple of games where you actu-ally threw the ball okay last year." I perked up at the sound of something positive. He was talking about a one-hitter I threw against the Yankees the same day Del Crandall, the new Brew-ers manager, arrived mid-season after Frank unceremoniously canned Dave Bristol by leaving his personal belongings out-side the locker room and having the gate guard block him from entering the clubhouse.

"You know what we need is more games like that and less conversations like this," he said, glancing over at a paper bag behind the desk that held his lunch, day-old tuna by its smell.

Frank looked at me and asked, "Are you married?"

I said, "Yes," fearing that I was going to get a lecture on mar-riage or infidelity or something out of the Book of Mormon next. "Good . . . very good, a man your age can get into trouble doing so much sitting around in all those hotel rooms," he said.

"Does she go to the games?"

"Yes," I answered wondering where this was going, adding "not to all of them because it cost $5 for the parking lot." I smiled inwardly for making a point in an attempt at redirecting the discussion. He paused, apparently pondering the price of parking at the stadium. "You know those prices are going up next year to $7.50." I slumped into the seat farther, feeling completely lost now and somewhat defeated. Exactly where he wanted me.

"Tell you what I'm going to do . . . and please consider this as a 'one-time only' offer. I will renew your salary, same minimum level and, for a measure of goodwill—and I want there to be goodwill between me and my players—I'll throw in a parking lot pass so your lovely wife can come to all of the games and see you win a few more of them this year than you did last year." He pushed the contract towards me. "Sign it, or the offer goes away when you leave this room," he said and rolled the capless pen towards me for a signature. I signed it and ran towards the parking lot that I wasn't going to have to pay for all next year.

****

In 1970, Curt Flood challenged the reserve clause, refusing to report to the Philadelphia Phillies. He filed a lawsuit against MLB claiming that his freedom in the labor market was restricted by the reserve clause. Heard by the U.S. Supreme Court, Flood lost the battle because of baseball's exemption from the antitrust law, but his fight began a war that led to a major victory for future players.

In 1972, on April Fool's Day, bad karma led to the first modern-day baseball strike, a thirteen-day affair that erased eighty-six games at the beginning of the season. The sole issue was the funding of the players' pension plan. The strike ended when the union and the owners settled on a $500,000 contribution to the plan, $100,000 more than originally offered. Called a clear winner for the owners on paper, it was a morale boost for the players union.

I was the Milwaukee Brewers player representative, responsible for keeping the players updated on the daily negotiations while communicating their concerns back to the union. This was an easy task because, since no one was being paid, a number of players were either camping out or joining us for makeshift dinners in our small condo at the time.

From 1972 on, every four-year round of negotiations during my career produced either a strike or a lockout. A couple of years later, Jim "Catfish" Hunter of the Oakland Athletics agreed with club owner Charles O. Finley that $50,000, half of Hunter's 1974 salary, would be placed into an insurance trust. Back in 1972, the farsighted Miller had negotiated a provision for arbitrating the players' grievances with the owners. When Finley failed to pay the $50,000 in a timely fashion, Hunter became a free agent. Hunter signed a five-year contract with the New York Yankees for $3.75 million, showing the salary clout that a free agent had in the labor market.

CHAPTER 14
MOVING ON

California Angels, 1974

BACK IN THE land of milk and honey, I pitched myself to a 2–6 record with the California Angels, doing more damage to the various buffets after the game than to the batter during the game. Despite Nolan Ryan's stellar individual performance, the Angels posted only 74 wins in a last-place showing in the AL West, and I became as expendable as last week's guacamole salad.

My market value was marginalized by very limited game time and the two-inning ditty I pitched in Oakland towards the end of the season. Jumping on my first pitch, Jesús Alou laid down a drag bunt. Covering first base, I stumbled slightly as I crossed the bag and pulled a hamstring. The team was so indifferent to my future pitching prospects that, rather than put me on the disabled list, they let me leave the team early to start classes for my junior year at Emerson College in Boston "to further my education." "You'll probably need it," were the final words of advice from Dick Williams, the Angels manager.

Baseball had been my life since I was a little boy. I practiced and dreamed big dreams. I'd picture myself in the act of playing before I actually got the opportunity. For most of my life, my vision quest was pretty successful. In the words of Julius Caesar: *Veni, vidi, vici*. I came, I saw, I conquered. I never realized how important envisioning success was until I sat on the bench for a whole season and watched the positive images fade away. I knew I would have to work hard to regain that forward-thinking focus as I continued to cling to my dream.

New York Yankees
Spring Training, 1975

Over the winter, I was traded to the New York Yankees. I first learned about the trade when a local Boston sports reporter called to ask my reaction to it. A few weeks later I received a letter from the Yankees that read: "We would like to offer you a contract and an invitation to join the team in spring training in Ft. Lauderdale, Florida." It went on to describe a split contract salary arrangement, not atypical of a player in my situation. The pay would be $20,000 salary if I made the club and $1,500 a month if I didn't and was assigned to play in the minors.

I was going to be a Yankee. To me, a new team signified a new chance to succeed. The possibility of not making the team never entered my mind. However, when I arrived in Fort

Lauderdale, I found a chorus line of pitchers lined up for a position in that rotation, including my old roommate, the Yankees' newest acquisition from free agency, Catfish Hunter.

Spring training is a little boy's dream come true. Spring training with the New York Yankees was Disneyland with all the trappings. I tried to hide the excitement I felt as I passed by the mirrors again to check it out. On the first day, I fell into an easy conversation with my locker neighbor Catfish. Ten years prior we had been featured on a Topps baseball gum card along with two other A's rookies, Rene Lachemann and Johnny Lee "Blue Moon" Odom. I'm guessing that baseball card is worth some money today.

Compared to the dusty makeshift spring training facilities in Tempe, Arizona, and El Centro, California, walking on to the NY Yankees spring training clubhouse was like walking onto a field of dreams. Unfortunately for me, I was spending more time dreaming about being on the field than walking out to the mound. Bill Virdon, who would be replaced by Billy Martin mid-season, was the manager. Bill and I had what you might call a "cordial, no-contact" spring training. We passed a couple of times in the locker room; he was usually on his way to the john, and I was unusually on my way to sit in the bullpen. Both of us spent more time sitting than playing.

The game of baseball treats some with kindness and ruthlessly mangles the lives of others. It tames raw talent and preys upon raw meat. The MVP of one series might be a persona non grata of the next. In the mind of the manager, you will always be only as good as your last performance. A career can hang on the outcome of a hanging curve. My career was on the chopping blocks, and I didn't see the cleaver coming.

To secure a spot on a major league ball club, you have to be all in. You need to draw a deaf ear to the sounds of discontent. No doubts. No excuses. Your focus has to be one hundred percent forward . . . fast-forward. Because of the extreme self-confidence that's necessary to suit up and take the field, a player hardly ever has the peripheral vision to see around the corners. The concentration and determination needed to perform great feats in the moment greatly decreases one's ability to look into the foreseeable future. The tedium of spring calisthenics and split-squad workouts and B team road games were just part of the drill. I was not pitching as often as I would like, but when I did get the chance, I felt my fastball was spinning nicely into shape.

Unbeknownst to me, once the Yankees serendipitously secured the services of Catfish Hunter, there was no room left in the starting rotation for me, and I no longer fit into the Yankees' plans. Despite my offseason preparation and my spring training success I was ruthlessly released on the last day of spring training—the day when every other club was trying to shrink their roster, a day when the timing of hooking up with another club was all but zero.

One of the Yankees' spring training mainstays was a priest named Fr. Joe Dispenza, the locker room chaplain and self-proclaimed personal confessor for player shenanigans and secrets which, if released, could have made him a very wealthy cleric. Father Joe, with his Roman collar, black suit, and big toothy mischievous grin, was a welcome fixture around the clubhouse. Spring training was a busy time for Father Joe. Many players were away from their families. The pressure of the season was off for players who had long-term contracts. Father Joe was the consummate insider, cognizant of what was happening on and off the field. He was famous for making the sign of the cross over an outfielder's head, forgiving him for a 0 for 4 the day before and a plethora of other lapses.

Father Joe and I planned on going out for dinner before we broke camp to celebrate my making the team . . . a "consecration of the grapes," he called it. I was overjoyed to be in Yankee pinstripes and back on the big stage for an encore. Father Joe knew everyone in the restaurant, all the patrons, all the wait staff. The drinks flowed freely. Father Joe rose for a brief benediction over the food. He started out by raising his glass and announcing that Jesus turned water into wine as his first public miracle. He, therefore, felt it was a fitting tribute to use this venerable fruit of the vine as a symbolic turning of the 1975 season into a pennant winner for the Yankees. He ended with a prayer. Everything ended in a prayer. "Please bow your heads," he said. He held out his arm like Jesus parting the water, "the wine in this glass symbolizes the blood that our Savior shed for our sins. The color of the wine also symbolizes the sweat that will be necessary for a Yankee pennant this year. The sweetness of the wine is but a forebearer to the sweet victory that will be ours at the end of the season." He took a taste and looked back over the patrons in the restaurant, who were held in his spell. "It is the chalice of life and the water of hope, and it has been shed for us so that Peppi can hit for the cycle against the Dodgers and Reggie can swing for the fences against Cleveland and so that the Yankees can have another ticker tape parade down Broadway next October." He paused a moment for effect. He worked a story like the Maestro at Carnegie Hall and said, "Salute. I mean, Amen." The room erupted in joy.

The phone rang on the end of the bar as a chorus of cheers and laughter careened through the restaurant. A telephone was on its way to the table. On the end of the line was the president and general manager for the Yankees. He was trying to find me. He had heard that Father Joe and I were going out to eat and surmised that we would be at Father Joe's favorite haunt. I took the phone from the waitress. The GM was direct. They didn't have room for two pitchers whose job it was to carry water in the middle innings. He knew that I wanted to get a chance to pitch for someone this year. They didn't want to hold me back since I had had such a fine spring and had proven myself a true professional and leader. I was surprised that the bullshit wasn't seeping into the Alfredo. He cut to the chase. "We're letting you go rather that option you to the minors where we don't think you'll be happy." He added that there was some paperwork that I needed to sign before I went on to the waiver wire, so he would have his assistant have the necessary forms ready. *Click.*

Baseball is all about leverage, and at the time, my leverage was limited to the few drops of wine left in my glass. Numb and vulnerable, I let Father Joe, irate at what he was overhearing, vent for me. I stayed quiet and listened. Sometimes in the middle of chaos, a person can impeach the angels for help, while other times reaching for a bottle of house Chianti can do the job. This situation called for both. Whatever my next step would be, I knew I better step up to the plate pretty quick. Suddenly my momentum was taking me back in the batter's box.

Father Joe was a new school priest with an old school persona like Guido Sarducci, the chain-smoking priest with tinted eyeglasses who appeared on *Laugh-In*. Joe wore a Roman collar, but I'm sure he had a .357 magnum tucked in his cassock somewhere. He knew everyone, including the working girls in the area. Of course, he knew the owners, having baptized two of their children and given Last Rites to a bar patron choking on a chunky hors d'oeuvre. I was going to need Father Joe's insight to help with my situation.

I asked the waiter, Emilio, to bring back the phone. It was three hours earlier in Oakland. "Hello," I said to the switchboard operator. "I'd like to speak to Mr. Finley."

"I'm not sure if he is here at the moment. Who may I say is calling?" I was half expecting the switchboard to direct me to an answering machine but instead was connected to Ruth Nidgen, Charlie Finley's longtime admin who just happened to be at her desk.

"Hi," she said, trying to place the name and, more important, the reason for the call.

"Hi, Ruth. Long time no see."

"Yes," she confirmed.

"I'm getting cut loose by the Yankees. They want me to sign option papers tonight. It's the last day of spring training, and I was hoping to speak to Charlie about hooking on with the A's." You could tell she was writing everything down, clarifying certain points and getting a number to call.

"Stay right where you are," she said, "I'm sure Charlie will want to talk to you."

The enigmatic Charlie Finley was the owner of the A's, the team I had originally signed with in 1964. Charlie was the first to believe in me, right out of high school. Charlie had a well-deserved reputation of being hard to contact unless of course you've just been released by the Yankees and Charlie could figure out a way to make a buck or two. More importantly, he relished the idea of giving a little *gotcha* to an organization that, in his opinion, had stolen his all-star pitcher.

The phone call came quickly. It rang on the phone that was perched in the booth's red leather tufted cushions.

Charlie Finley was on the phone. He said, "I heard good stories about your pitching this spring."

I responded with, "Let me tell you a little about what happened." Chopping six weeks into six sentences, I finished with an up-sell phrase, "I just need a place to prove myself again. I know I can help someone." All pabulum Charlie has heard before, but he liked me, he knew I would follow his instructions, and he was anxious to get back at the Yankees.

"Where are you?" was the next question. "Where are you at this very minute?" The questions came fast and furious.

Yes, I could get a ride to the airport. No, I would not, under any circumstances, go back to the hotel or the ballpark. Alright, I would leave immediately and assume another identity for the next week or so.

His last words were, "Do exactly as I tell you, and I will assure you that if you pitch well, I'll get you back in the bigs again this year. Maybe not with the A's, but somewhere you can make a difference."

The trust was implicit and also irreplaceable. I didn't have another option. The plan that Charlie had outlined on the phone felt like the plot of a cheap spy novel. What he would gain by signing me was small change on the IOU Charlie figured he was owed by the Yankees, but it was at least a little thorn he could rub in their sides.

Regrettably leaving my last spoonful of spumoni in the bowl, I bolted out of the restaurant and headed to the airport. At the airport, a one-way plane ticket was waiting for me to Phoenix, Arizona. Ruth had included a page of instructions. I was to register at the Holiday Inn under the name of Johnson. The room was already paid for. I was not to show any ID. I was to order room service for my meals and stay away from restaurants for one week. At that point, Charlie would call me with further instructions.

Following his instructions to a tee, I traveled under the name Johnson and hid in a Phoenix hotel for five days, enough time for the wire option period to expire. Charlie then claimed me without having to pay the usual $25,000 acquisition fee. Since New York was unable to get my signature, they had no other choice but to release me, making me a free agent. The rules of baseball were quirky, and Charlie was the chair of the committee that had drawn up this rule at the winter meetings. There's a good chance he might have been the only owner who was aware of the new rule.

Mr. Finley called Mr. Johnson's room at the end of the week. He was pleased that his plan had played out the way he intended. "Hey listen, thanks for helping me stick it to those bastards. I enjoyed fucking them more than the money," Charlie said, before offering me a spot on the Pacific Coast League's AAA team, the Tucson Toros. No promises were given, but no promises were needed.

Tucson, Arizona

After being hidden away for a week, not knowing where I was or even who I was, getting back into uniform was just what the doctor ordered. Finley picked Tucson because of manager Hank Aguirre. Hank was a former player and a manager from the old school, an "old hand." A lean lefty, Hank had pitched for four different teams. The majority of his sixteen years were spent in Detroit, pitching mostly in relief. Hank was my mentor and guide. He communicated in a way that made hard things sound simple.

When I arrived in Tucson, Hank asked me, "Do you want to start or relieve?" I told him I just wanted to pitch. I told him I believed that relievers usually had one foot already out the door on most clubs.

"That's true," he said, "but there's a big need for someone who can throw hard every couple of days and get a guy out in a crucial situation."

The minor leagues are different than the bigs. One player said, "It's like a pond full of guppies." The Pacific Coast League (PCL) had bigger guppies than most minor leagues, and every individual guppy was strutting his colors and anxiously awaiting a chance to shine. No one wanted to stay there a day longer than they had to, and everyone was hoping for a ticket to the Show. It was like a doctor's waiting room—you took a number and hoped it wouldn't be too long before you're called. Clubs used the PCL as a revolving door, ushering players back and forth as injuries and performance on the big league level dictated. A thin veil of civility circled around the desperate players. It's put up or go home.

Tucson was hot . . . blazing hot. Shuffling into the sauna-like clubhouse, I recognized some friendly voices. The affable Lew Krausse was holding court near the hot tub where catcher Charlie Sands was trying to soak out a few "burrs" on his inner calf muscles, a reminder of the 3-2 loss they suffered the day before. A practical joke was underway, and Lew's jokes were not to be interrupted.

"Hello Skipper," he said to me sarcastically. "Nice of you to join us here in hell." A big leaguer in the minor leagues feels like parking in the short-term lot. A minor leaguer in the bigs worries about being towed. "I heard a rumor that you were coming here last week; where were you?" Lew asked. I told Lew about the Yankees, my conversation with Charlie, and my past week in

Phoenix. We both knew Charlie was a man of honor and, more importantly, a man of his word. Lew offered his own brand of advice. "You can reinvent yourself in the desert sands. You can be any damn thing you want to be . . . Just pick one." In light of the available options opened to me, I chose to become a closer.

For six years I'd thrown round baseballs towards round bats with the ardent hope that they missed everything in their path. I'd even been paid for this pleasure and had been performing this feat in places I barely remembered. In the parlance of sports, I was a journeyman, a visitor of many lands, an infielder converted to pitching because of poor hitting, a starting pitcher converted to relief pitching because of failure to go deep into the game. However, a journey is never over until the final destination is reached. In Tucson, I discovered something about myself and about how I pitched, and that discovery led me to a new road less traveled.

Some conversions in my career have come evolutionarily and some made out of necessity. My conversion to a closer, which occurred in the heat of the Arizona desert, was more of an epiphany than an epitaph. I was pitching short relief. Short, meaning not too many innings. Relief, meaning not starting. And it was working out much better than I envisioned.

A less than stellar stint with the Angels and a shockingly star-crossed spring training with the Yankees had seriously shaken my faith in my baseball future. Landing in Tucson, Arizona, was both a curse and a blessing. I had been playing baseball for years, but I still had a lot to learn about the psychology of relief pitching. A central piece in my mental development in Tucson was triggered by my catcher, Charlie Sands. Charlie played the game hard, old-school style. I don't think I fully understood what was going on inside my mind until I brainstormed with Charlie. He clarified my new role and my new responsibilities.

Charlie was my roommate on road trips. We spent many nights conversing about the game within the game. One conversation that struck a chord with me was the idea that pitching was basically communication. In the middle of all the confusion on the field and beyond the tumult of fans' conversations, beyond the sixteen vendors in the bleachers throwing peanut bags around, beyond the waves of enthusiasm sweeping through the cheap seats, if you looked closely, a narrow band of communication was underway. A message was crafted by the sender, sent through a channel, received by a source. The message might look ordinary, nonplussed, professional, and captured. But staring down the barrel, it was imperative to deliver a clear shot. These discussions led me to resolve to become a different pitcher, a closer.

It might sound crazy but, for me, every day was a new baseball adventure. Every baseball was a little different, and sometimes I forgot how the seams on the ball felt. I'd squeeze the ball to see if it would move. I'd forget how the arm breezed through the air. I'd forget how the toe of the left foot found the dirt before the heel. I'd forget how the fingertips released the ball like little catapults. I'd forget the wrist cock and the lead arm position pointing at the target. Every day was a new day. It was time I concentrated on remembering.

Every player prepares to play in his own way and on his own schedule. I preferred to get to the park early and often was the last to leave. My manager Hank, fellow pitcher Leo Mazzone, and I usually were the first to arrive at the ballpark. We'd kill some time with a gin rummy game in the clubhouse and then head out to the field to loosen up, stretch, and toss a few soft warmup throws—a mini rehearsal before the rest of the guys got there.

One afternoon while playing catch with Leo Mazzone, a diminutive left-handed reliever, sharing a light game of toss and the same minor league sentence in Tucson, something strange happened. It started as I was throwing a few soft ones to warm up. The ball arced through the afternoon heat and landed with a soft thud in Leo's glove. He threw it back. I always play a game with myself even while playing simple toss. I always hit the glove as if it was being held at shoulder height. Nothing left, nothing right, never bouncing the ball. Today was no exception.

It's all part of remembering, reigniting the sources inside. Practice was never meaningless. These tosses were rehearsals. I tossed the third ball with a little more on it, loosening up as we played catch. I hinged my glove hand at the wrist exaggeratedly just to make the tossing feel a little different. And it did. The ball sailed with a darting motion right to left and nearly missed Leo's glove. He made the adjustment just in time, preventing the ball from going off into the outfield.

It was just toss after all, but today the ball seemed to have a mind of its own. The ball was hot and alive, darting and

189

making noise, tearing through the leather webbing of Leo's glove. The second throw was more like mid-game than mid-afternoon. "Christ, what the f . . . !" Leo said. "Take a little off . . . What are you trying to prove?" I didn't know the answer, but the ball felt light and responsive like all it needed was a little nudge, and it would do the rest. I was taking a little bit off, but the ball didn't seem to care. For the next few weeks, I would wrestle with several adjustments in my windup and pray that the new life in my fastball would still be there the next day.

Day after day the life was not only there, it was getting better. The whole sense of reality was confounding. I was standing on the mound with almost unhittable gas. *Just find the plate,* I told myself. The league was listening. I had something no one else possessed and was rock sure the big leagues would hear the echo. When things change, you have to adjust and learn how to be at home in your own skin. After striking out as a big league infielder, it was "strongly suggested" by the powers that be that I become a pitcher. I was force-fed the mechanics of throwing a fastball in instructional league and secured a role as a starting pitcher the following spring. I became what a scout would refer to as a one-pitch pitcher. I mostly threw a fastball or, as my teammate George Scott described, "a heater." My raw talent could have definitely benefited from a little refinement. I threw the ball hard, but I hardly ever knew where the ball would end up. I pitched opening day in Milwaukee twice. I pitched back-to-back one-hitters against Oakland and Baltimore. My catchers, teammates, coaches, and managers could never understand why my record wasn't more successful. The fans just shook their heads. I guess I was more promise than performance.

Transitioning from a starter to a closer, in my sixth professional season as a pitcher, I had spent the last few months in the minor leagues with the Tucson Toros. As I closed in on the psychology and physiology of a closer, a whole new world of opportunity opened up. One journalist in Arizona described me as "a pitcher who found religion in the desert sands of the Tucson bullpen." By mid-summer, I knew I would be heading back to the big leagues. That renewed faith in my fastball helped me to leave the desert sands of Tucson for the concrete jungle of New York.

Call Waiting

Sleeping off a bit of a hangover, the call I'd been waiting for came in the blur of a hazy Arizona scorcher. It came through the landline in a musty old motel in Phoenix on a road trip. Pitching short relief for the Tucson Toros, I had thrown two innings the night before and snagged my twelfth save of the month, a new Pacific Coast League record. My wife had joined me on the trip, and we had been up late celebrating on the balcony of the motel. Not having heard the phone ring the next morning, I was more than a little annoyed at being urgently shaken to wake up. Finley was on the line. The clock read 8:21 am, Mountain Time. Charlie Finley, the owner of the Oakland A's and the Toros AAA franchise, wasn't calling for small talk. As promised, Charlie was calling with a deal.

This phone call signaled a date with the future, a new team, a new MLB uniform, and a chance to wrestle personal demons and doubts lingering in the dark corners of my mind. The local news headlines in cities left behind had excoriated me as a mediocre pitcher, "not good enough to be a star, not bad enough to headline a trade." They said I had "a career filled with little luck and bad bounces." Luck, if there had been any at all, was hard to find in the lopsided losses of the Milwaukee Brewers. Bad bounces were more a topic in south side Milwaukee barrooms where I was frequently the subject of many beer brandishes and chastened by sharp-penned writers and pithy announcers reporting the game and sparing no punches. But in the last two months, everything had changed rather unexpectedly.

The events of this season fell into two halves: one half too unpredictable to be a melodrama, the other too preposterous to be fiction. And although the last act had not been written yet, the facts were simple—my baseball career, which was destined for summer stock three months ago, was now moving to Broadway.

CHAPTER 15
NEW YORK, NEW YORK, 1975

THE 1975 NATIONAL League East Pennant was speeding along fast and furious in the race to the finish line. The excitement of being in the hunt trumped any feeling I ever had before. There was enough tension in the locker room to wrap around the City of New York. Herbie Norman took his position as clubhouse manager seriously and did all that he could to add some comic relief to the tension. He constantly invented ways to play little tricks on everyone. Having someone like Herbie around was a blessing, unless of course you happened to be the father of the relief player bearing the brunt of the jokes.

More than a decade after leaving my childhood home, I felt I had finally found a home-away-from-home with the Mets. I pitched well enough to win a secure spot in the bullpen. And when the opportunity opened to appear late in the game, I pitched more than well enough and established myself as the closer. My family was overjoyed that I was back in the

Northeast, especially my father, Claude. The drive from Norwood, Massachusetts, was within striking distance of New York and most weekends would find Dad cruising down I-95 and crossing over the Whitestone Bridge into Flushing.

The Mets reportedly had a closed clubhouse, open only to players and press. There was an engraved sign on the door stating that the league prohibited unauthorized entry. I soon discovered that this rule was not really all that etched in stone. By the end of a solid week, I asked Herbie if it were possible for my father to come into the clubhouse. He said, "Wow that would be wonderful, I'd love to meet your dad. It would be great if he could come down for a game and come in here to meet all the players." So we made plans for the following Saturday. Having followed me to visiting clubhouses around the league, Dad was anxious to visit the home clubhouse and to see where I worked. I worked pretty hard on that particular Saturday. I pitched the last two innings of the game and got a save.

Ever since driving me down to my debut at the Polo Grounds in 1962, Dad had a love/hate relationship with New York. He loved the stage on which players played in New York, but hated the highways and byways one needed to navigate to get there. A nervewracking ride down I-95 was followed by a confusing circumnavigation of the Shea parking lot. After walking halfway around the stadium to finally find the will call window, and halfway back again to find the players entrance, Dad tentatively approached the "Players Only" sign at the entrance to the clubhouse. Dad wasn't comfortable ignoring signs. He introduced himself to the security officer in the vestibule and made his way through the next door into the main locker room. Normally Dad's demeanor was unassuming and today it was bordering on cold-footed timidity. He was clearly out of his element. He took about five steps in, onto the carpeted floor of the clubhouse.

Herbie Norman came running over and confronted Dad: "Who are you? We don't allow strangers in this part of the building. Who the fuck let you in here?" Dad was raised not to swear. He raised his children not to swear. In his world swearing was "not necessary in civil conversation." Now, Dad never cursed, and when someone else conversed in such an uncivil manner, it caused him to shrink back further into his shell.

"Well, I don't know," he stammered. "I'm Skip Lockwood's dad," he uttered apologetically. "Skip said it would be alright if I came into the clubhouse today and waited for him after the game. He said he cleared it with the clubhouse manager."

Herbie played his role to a tee, and Dad was unwittingly playing right into his hand. "I'm the fucking clubhouse manager, and I never heard of anything like this. We don't let anyone in here who doesn't hold press credentials." Herbie was in his glory. "I'm going to lose my job," he said. "I've got to do something with you before the brass gets down here." Herbie looked around to gauge his options. "Quick," he said, "in this office." He motioned to Dad to go into the bat closet, which was filled with boxes of new bats, some loose older bats, and a few broken ones that would be used for batting practice. There was no chair and no artificial illumination. Ever compliant, my father did what he was told.

A few minutes later I came in from being interviewed on the postgame show. I scanned the locker room to find Dad. He was not sitting on my stool in front of my locker or in the chair near the food table. I asked Herbie, "Hey Herb, have you seen my father?" Herbie looked sheepish, a look I had seen before. He pointed to the closet in the corner, the bat closet. *Oh no*, I said to myself. When I opened the door, Dad was standing in the dark, feeling very guilty that he was going to cost Herbie his job. I guess Dad and Herbie shared a strange sense of humor for, after a sincere apology and lots of laughter, the welcoming mat was open for Dad for the next five years.

The bullpen housed several veteran relievers and a couple of friends I had played with on other teams. Ken Sanders, a seasoned right-hander who relied on a hard slider and the ability to grind in the late innings, and I had pitched together in Milwaukee and Anaheim. Ken joined the Mets earlier in the year and was a top contender for the role of closer in the late innings. Soon after I arrived, Ken was pitching at Shea on a Sunday afternoon. It might be hard to imagine now in our 24/7 media coverage, but in the mid-seventies, not all games were televised and, at times, extra cameras were added, and a television camera was placed behind home plate on a rolling base so it could easily travel from one side of home plate to the other. A louvered door in the Plexiglas behind home plate allowed the camera nose to peek out.

Ken was pitching with a two-run lead when John Stearns threw the ball back to the mound. With Ken blinded by the sun reflecting off the louvered door, the ball hit him in the right eye, dropped him to his knees, knocked him down, and almost knocked him out. The trainer ran out to the field and called for the paramedics. A hushed silence filled the stadium as the players circled around as he was led off the field. After a stint on the disabled list, the "Bulldog" returned to the bullpen, but he continued to suffer from double vision for the remainder of the season. Ken's injury put the role of closer up for grabs within the Mets bullpen. Ultimately, I won the part. A strange twist of fate had sidelined my friend and skyrocketed my career.

****

Every quality pitcher I ever met focused completely on preparedness, mentally and physically. Jim Palmer in his book *The Art of Pitching* shared, "When I was pitching good I could almost see where the ball would go before I threw it." At the top of his game, Sandy Koufax talked about pitching as being an extension of his body. From my personal perspective, the best pitcher in the National League, and maybe the best pitcher in all of baseball, was Tom Seaver. Immensely talented, Tom was a student of the game. He believed that the velocity, movement, and location of your pitches could vary greatly from outing to outing. Even a talented, dedicated pitcher will inevitably have to endure a slump. A pitcher needed to battle his way through it and limit the damage to a game or two.

When you start to struggle, you should analyze your motion in a mirror. A pitcher must be sufficiently objective to detect and compensate for these differences. He believed that averages always favored a pitcher, but that a good hitter sometimes will hit good pitching. He stressed certain things—avoid walks, get the first out of an inning, don't let the batter make contact with the meat of the bat, and don't let the batter claim both sides of the plate.

I had trouble handling my emotions in between innings. Typically, I would come in from an inning and pace the runway leading to the locker room until I got a chance to go back out. The whole process of trying to stay so "up" was exhausting, and I was having difficulty throwing strikes when I returned to the mound. Every pitcher has to find his own method of dealing with time between innings. A passive-aggressive starter with the Pilots liked to spend the time glaring out at his opponents. A pitcher with the Brewers opted to play cards down in the runway. One of my Angels teammates meditated in between innings. I asked Seaver what he did. Tom reminded me of an old childhood game we played in the schoolyard, red light/green light. He said that when he went out to the mound and crossed the foul line, he said green light to himself, meaning that it's time to step on the gas. When he walked off the mound in between innings, he'd call red light, foot off the gas, to himself. So in between innings, he was off duty.

Late in the season, the Mets were in Chicago for a mid-week series with the Cubs. The game was scheduled as an afternoon game, and the phone in my hotel room rang at nine o'clock in the morning, the familiar voice on the other end of the line demanding that I get my butt out of bed. "We're going to the Art Institute to see something you will never forget," beckoned Seaver. "Meet you in the lobby in twenty minutes."

Tom was a complicated person with many diverse interests. One was wine, which he has successfully pursued with great passion after his baseball career. He collected dirt from the various fields in the league for research. He studied various forms of art, and he loved going to museums around the league. We decided that in the time remaining in the season he and I were going to see as many museums as we could fit in.

We hailed a cab. Tom directed, "The Art Institute of Chicago." The Chicago Art Institute had acquired a masterpiece of Claude Monet, *Water Lilies*. Seaver was my museum guide. We wound our way up to the third floor, which was dedicated to this one work of art. The inscription underneath the painting said, "One instant, one aspect of nature contains it all." Monet produced this enormous mural at his home in Giverny. The mural was really a series of murals with a single, timeless motif, a single focal point flower garden, or a smaller pond spanned by a Japanese footbridge. Seaver studied this painting in college, and he was intrigued to see it in person. We turned the corner, and the Monet stood before us. A museum guide related: "In his first water-lily series, Monet painted the pond environment, with its water lilies, bridge, and trees neatly divided by a fixed horizon. Over time, he became less and less concerned with conventional pictorial space. By the time he painted his third group of these works, he had completely done away with the horizon line altogether."

Tom stopped to see if I was paying attention, and the guide continued. "He created something called a spatially ambiguous canvas—as if he was looking down at it, focusing solely on the surface of the pond, with its cluster of plants floating amidst the reflection of sky and trees." It was incredibly beautiful. Blues were vivid. The water was moving. I felt like I was dripping wet inside the canvas. The whole thing was alive. It took my breath away. We sat on one of the benches in front. Other patrons clustered behind. Always a relative concept, time appeared to stand still. I was lost in the moment.

Tom woke me up, "We've got to get going back. In this arena, it might be fine to contemplate the relativity of time, but if we don't make it to the stadium for warmups, we'll both be fined." Tom in his own way painted a canvas, one that was bounded by bases and wooden fences less spatially indifferent. Seaver believed that a fastball needed dimension and depth. It needed to be thrown through the catcher, not to the catcher.

****

September 28, 1975

The early September surging for the New York Mets 1975 season sputtered to an end with an 82-80 record and a third-place finish in the National League's Eastern Division. A bedraggled group, battle-weary and tired, arrived in Philadelphia with well-worn baseball gear, golf clubs in travel bags, personal items marked for destinations all over the country, and X-rays in oversized brown envelopes to consult with doctors back home. The visiting team looked much like a traveling circus about to pull up the tents.

Even in the best of seasons, ones where the race is close right down to the last day and each and every game matters right down to the last pitch, the last few games can drag. Many players just want the pressure to be over. Innings can turn into protracted affairs with managers spending too much time on the field, commercials soaking up energy, and a momentary lack of concentration spoiling the whole year. Mostly players don't want to get hurt, and they really don't want to be embarrassed by their final performance. Some players tough it out through nagging injuries. Others already have needed surgeries scheduled right after the season is over. However, for a few more hours they all will dig deep, muster hidden motivation, and give it everything they've got left.

Change became the new normal during the course of that season. The twenty-five-man roster saw more than its share of changes that season. Sixteen pitchers made their appearance in the Mets lineup. Yogi Berra, legendary New York catcher known to be the heart and soul of the Yankees for years, began the season as the Mets manager but, falling victim to a mediocre group effort mid-season, gave way to Roy McMillan. Uncertainty had become commonplace. Emotions ran rampant. For the final game, the team would take the field running on fumes and playing purely for pride.

And no one was more proud than the right-hander and future Hall of Fame member named Tom Seaver. With a win that day, Seaver would statistically outdistance Randy Jones of San Diego in the Cy Young race. Tension was taut in the clubhouse. Batting practice, the usual freewheeling cushion before the raw emotion of the game, was canceled by both teams. It left a vacancy that was being filled with nervous energy. I had a pretty good inclination that I was going to be a participant in today's festivities and couldn't wait for the game to begin.

Fan responses would be magnified. Cheers would be louder. Boos would be protracted. Oh yes . . . and my one-year contract would end with the game that day.

****

The feeling usually hits me as soon as I wake up. I jolt into a sitting position even though I'm mostly still asleep. I'm not choking; that will come later. It must have been a bad dream. I shiver as a sense of enormity sweeps past me. I see a clock with no time left and a pitcher standing on the mound with a ball in his hand.

For the last ten years the feelings before, during, and after the game haven't changed. The anxiety is still there, but now it's manageable. The fear that used to be paralyzing is now under control. And, more importantly, the actual playing of the game is much more predictable. What has changed is my approach to all of the above.

I have what can best be described as a routine. Sometimes it works better than others, but it always works, and I have come to rely on it. Right now my emotions are in motion, bordering on being out of control. It's no time to sit around.

Game-day anxiety builds in intensity, and if I don't have a plan for each and every time the anxiety shows up, I'll end up hugging the commode. I've discovered that a mantra can help. I say, "bring in on," a phrase that I will repeat hundreds of times today.

From where I stand, the final outcome is worth dealing with the little nerves right now. I have to cope with the pregame stuff but, once the game starts, the action of the game and the adrenaline will take care of the rest. So all I have to do is to get into the game and the jitters should be history. We'll see.

The first wave of fear surfaces during lunch in the hotel restaurant. Lunch is usually breakfast for me—eggs, toast, and stuff, but no meat before I play. Fans might assume that professional athletes, with all the games they play and all the big crowds, would not get nervous, but nothing could be farther from the truth. The thing, and I mean the only thing, that professional athletes have is history. The future has to become your friend, not your enemy.

Indios trainer Nelson Decker years ago said that in order to get a hold on my emotions it would be wise to watch a movie of me playing, to remove myself from the present and go into the future. I do this by picturing myself frame by frame—sort of a game video timeline with me floating about it, safe and secure. Nelson said that emotions flow around and around in concentric circles, as if they were swirling water inside a drinking cup. He cautioned that even though you may feel like you're over the jitters for the moment, they will keep coming around again with more intensity the closer you get to the game, touching all the same feeling points of emotion, anxiety, and fear.

"Don't try to stop them or mask them, because that would be futile," he would say. And no matter how many times or how many years have passed, I still face the exact same fears, the armada of dread.

****

Once the game started, it was apparent Seaver did not have his usual sharpness. He was missing a little from side to side on the plate—not much, but enough to get uncharacteristically behind on a few batters. Six innings later and with rounded shoulders, he headed for the Mets bench to become part of the sideline for a few tense innings.

****

My warmup throws are completed with lightning speed. I'm pleased to have life in my fastball and command of the plate, at least in the bullpen. However, the bullpen session is just a warmup, a chance to get the muscles loose, nothing more.

It's the bottom of the sixth inning. I enter the game with a man on third, nobody out, and a two-run lead. As a relief pitcher, coming into any game carries a lot of anxiety, but coming into this game, a game that means so much to Tom Seaver, to the New York Mets, and to my own future career, is a new level of every emotion in the books. As I step on the mound, I feel as small as an ant. The enormity of the ballpark hits me. It's like I am the only player on the field. The waves of crowd noises seem to rise and crash into me like the roar of the ocean. Filaments of light creep through the upper deck, turning the field into a pastoral landscape. Any other person on earth would be able to enjoy the scene. It's anything but tranquil standing on this pitcher's mound in the middle of New York's last game of the season.

I wonder if the older couple on the plane with me a few months ago when I first arrived in New York is now visiting Philadelphia. Maybe they're at the game. I can't allow my mind to wander. I say "bring in on." This saying is meant to give me a feeling of being settled, being comfortable with the chaos around me. And it works. Immediately a new calm engulfs me, a feeling that I can command the ball, command the strike zone, and, in turn, command the outcome of the game to replace the doubt. I plan for this to happen. I plan for the stadium to feel big, for the crowd to seem loud. I plan to feel small. This is the first of many emotions that I will overcome today before the game is over. I will feel over-whelmed again and again today. The words "bring in on" will continue to be my mantra.

Staring in at my first series of signs, I pull my cap down. The brim is wet. Good, I'll use it to moisten my fingers as the game goes on. I raise the glove so it's just the catcher and the target in my sight line. Michael Allen Anderson, the rugged center fielder, is digging a small hole in the righthand batter's box. I squeeze the seams on the ball. There is literally no room for any errors, no room for any mistakes. My fastball will be the pitch of choice today. The second fastball flies to center and scores Mike Schmidt from third. The score is now 5-4, in our favor. I get the ball back and rub the fly ball off it. It wasn't exactly a mistake. But the game is very tight now. Johnny Oates, taking over catching duties for the day and giving Bob Boone a break before the postseason starts, strikes out with a defensive passive wave on a fastball that splits the outside half of the plate. Greg Luzinski, the Bull to his teammates, strides to the plate with a sneer on his face. He digs some dirt out the batter's box looking much like his namesake. He settles in. His legs look like tree trunks. He takes a massive swing at the first pitch, intending to make it a souvenir for the right field bleacherites in the neighboring town. Two pitches later, chasing pitches that go gradually up the ladder, as the players would say, he strikes out, slamming the bat into the ground in disgust. The sixth inning is over and, more importantly, the lead is preserved.

The Mets fail to score in the top of the seventh. It looks like five runs might be the final day's output for us. I'm back on the mound before I have time to breathe in and out. The first thing I do when I get back to the rubber is to gasp in two large breaths of air. In the clubhouse about a week ago, Seaver and I were talking about the importance of breathing, which for me is the opposite of holding your breath. Breathing brings relaxation to the muscles, especially the one between my ears. For Seaver, nothing is left to chance. Breathing is deliberate, calculated, counted. On the mound, I center my breathing. I let the relaxation wash over me. Air brings life. Air brings balance.

In the bottom of the seventh, I start my warmup pitches by controlling my eyes as well as my pitches. I picture pitching clues that I have used over the years. Seaver says the good ones can see every pitch. The one I'm seeing looks like a bullwhip. I roll the tap and picture myself using the bullwhip and casting it towards the batter. It unfurls somewhat slowly but, by the time it's at the batter, it's snapping and biting. I hear it crack as the pitch lands in the catcher's mitt.

David Cash, Phillies All-Star second baseman, leads off. He strolls to the plate. I don't think he likes whips and, while he's standing there before he gets into the box, I want him to hear the bullwhip cracking. I stare in at his face. I want him to look out at the mound. He leads off the bottom of the seventh, taking one feeble swing, and strikes out. Perennial All-Star shortstop Larry Bowa goes after what turns out to be a very hittable curveball in the upper end of the zone. He pops up to Mets third baseman Roy Staiger. I exhale loudly when it comes down. I slap the side of my leg. I'm fortunate. After all, not all mistakes stay in the ballpark. Tom Hutton stands next in line. He has an unusual ability to hit Tom Seaver—hitting for an average of 3.20 in 62 plate appearances with 11 walks, 3 home runs, and 11 RBIs. He's a reserve infielder and is conscripted to play in this game precisely because Seaver was pitching. But now Seaver isn't pitching. A strange-looking character is standing out there wearing John Lennon glasses looking more like a history professor. This baseball history professor has a fastball in the high nineties and the attitude of a Doberman on too long a leash. Ron Hodges, the Mets catcher, pounds the mitt on the outside half of the plate. The last two pitches are heaters with late movement away from the hitter. Hutton strikes out. Two innings under my belt, two more to go.

In the top of the eighth, John Milner grounds out to shortstop, and Ron Hodges grounds out to second. I hit a slow roller to short and run medium slow to first, making the third out. The good *thing about the top of the eighth is I don't have time to feel much of anything. In what seems like two minutes I am back on the mound.*

Starting off the eighth inning is John William "Jay" Johnstone Jr., a left-handed batter later to be known as a prankster with the Dodgers, strolls toward home plate with a quizzical look on his face, in mocking disbelief that this bookish-looking individual can really be holding the mighty Phillies at bay on the last day of the season. He taps the plate, directing my attention. Jay is a centerpiece of the Phillies lineup, batting third in front of home run hitter Mike Schmidt. I get a curve over for the first strike and two consecutive fastballs in on his hands and by him, strikes two and three. If he could have heard me, he might have heard a "see ya" escape from my lips. We'll never know, but he strikes out in what even an outsider would say is rude treatment. Michael Jack Schmidt waits on deck. (Mike will be a twelve-time All-Star with 548 home runs before being voted into the Hall of Fame, and he is considered by many to be the best third baseman ever.) At the plate, Mike turns his back slightly to me. He is looking for a heater, which is what he is about to get, something he can park in the bleachers for his league-leading 39th homer of the year. He takes a sharp breaking curve for strike one and swings at another one in the dirt. He then takes two fastballs away and finally strikes out on a curve, which might have been ball three. Mike Rogodskinski, a light-hitting outfielder in what would be his last at-bat in the big leagues, hits my second pitch, which gets in on his hands for a weak pop-up to Mike Phillips at shortstop.

My third inning is in the books. Jumping the first base line for luck, I get back to the Mets bench in what could best be described as a competitive frenzy. I want to go back out there and finish the job. I am pacing back and forth. And then I remember that Seaver and I have talked about how "red light, green light" can manage the adrenaline in between innings. I remind myself of this stoplight analogy, take a deep breath, and let the tension wash away from my shoulders. Red light lets me save my energy. Held scoreless again in the ninth, the Mets are holding on to a one-run lead heading into the last half of the ninth inning.

It's go time again. For me, it's a time to establish myself as a pitcher of substance, a pitcher who can be counted on in high-stress situations—to establish myself as a "closer." I am running on fumes. The crowd noise has gotten suddenly, but noticeably, quieter. It's time to put everything that I know, everything I've worked on, into practice. I can feel my heart pulsating through the logo on the front of my uniform.

The fourth, fifth, and sixth batters in the lineup are due up and, to make things worse, this is their second look at me today, never a good thing for a relief pitcher. Can I relax enough to let the pitches roll off the tips of my fingers and find home plate with the same velocity I have so far all game? Can I maintain momentum? I take in another large gulp of air and blow it as far toward home plate as I can. The same level of pitching will not be good enough. I'm going to have to find another gear. I hinge my wrist back and forth like I'm shifting a race car. Mike Anderson, who hit a fastball to center to score a run during his previous at-bat, pops up my second pitch into foul ground for Ron Hodges to track down. Hodges does a good job squeezing it. He walks out to the mound with the baseball and firmly plants it into my glove. He says, "You got this. Don't think, just give me that heater." On the next pitch I slide forward into my landing position so easily it gives me a little extra on my fastball, and Johnny Oates flies to short right field. Veteran power hitter Garry Maddox, primarily known for his extraordinary defense, is pinch-hitting for Randy Lerch and strolls to the plate slowly. Sportswriter Ray Didinger, of Baseball Digest, *once said, "Two-thirds of the Earth is covered by water. The other one third by Garry Maddox." Garry has been sitting all day, but he knows what's going on. He is looking dead red, and he's going to get it.*

I get the count to two strikes. This is the moment I've been waiting for. This is the exact picture in my mind. All the effort, all the visualization drills, and all the practices on and off the field, all rolled up into one pitch . . . this pitch.

Like the little boy many years ago with big dreams, I feel a familiar expression wash over my face . . . more confident now than ever before. It's the face of control.

I grip the ball inside my glove, pressing it higher into my fingers and away from the palm.

My fingers tighten over the leather. Everything seems to fit better, more in line, clearer and focused. Time slows down.

I focus on my target, rotate forward, and pull down hard on the laces.

The last pitch of the Mets 1975 season takes off . . . and heads toward Gary Maddox, who is standing at a ready position in the batter's box.

It arches towards home plate . . . covering the distance between us in no time.

A pitch that was originally formed by a little boy's hope mixed with a little boy's belief that some things do come true . . . that pitch is now real and about to end the Mets season on a positive note.

The bat makes a silent swoosh, followed by the sound of the baseball hitting the leather in the catcher's mitt. I raise my hands to the sky and breathe in the victory.

On the mound stands a pitcher . . . a plan formed into reality and a pitch thrown with insight . . . an Insight Pitch.

CHAPTER 16
THE LAST HURRAH

Denver, Colorado, 1981

I **SWAY TOWARDS THE** *outfield, the domain of pregame pitchers during batting practice, arriving at my self-assigned position as batting practice commences. I hear the high-fives of the infielders fielding grounders in a group.*

I secure my usual haunt in left-center, halfway to the outfield fence. Non-game-day pitchers don't have much to do for the three hours before the game. I patrol the outfield sky. To me, batting practice is a chance to prepare. I play every ball that comes my way as a game situation. No ball is permitted to touch the ground. I've worked on this technique for fifteen years and took pride in my work. The other pitchers know to stay away. I call the ball when it leaves the bat. "I've got it," I bellow out time and again and it echoes in the empty stadium. Sometimes the cleanup crew, hosing down the seats, will howl with laughter. It doesn't bother me. I always play with purpose, and this is where it starts.

I patrol left center with my usual vengeance. Today is a good day. I've made two diving one-handers, a couple of sliders, a last-of-the-ninth-inning game-saver, and just one bent-knee shoe top scooper, followed with bullet throws to the batting practice bucket, nailing clumsy invisible runners who dare to test my throwing arm. I am an old fool getting the most out of what's left for me to play, getting dirty and getting the job done.

Today my concentration is a little off. "When are they going to call me up?" I keep asking myself. Five years ago it had been Tucson, this year Denver, next year who knows? I am standing in left-center in Mile High Stadium's outfield, dirty and sweating, hoping to finally drown out the cat-calls and howls that pepper my sleep as well as the locker room whispers and snickers. I am in Denver pitching for the cellar-dwelling Bears in the PCL, the result of a shoulder that stubbornly refuses to heal, even after two years in rehab, fifteen cortisone shots, hours of exercise therapy, and numerous attempts to pitch through the pain.

Halfway through batting practice, Brad, one of the honorary bat boys, runs over to me and says, "Nice catch. Felipe wants to see you in his office." Felipe is the Bears' manager, the head coach, and one of the three Alou brothers who played simultaneously in the major leagues. A soft-spoken, sensitive man, Felipe sings his words with smiling deliberate misuses and omissions. He is wise for his age, and I consider him a friend. I know that Felipe will have a big smile on his face and will give me a Denver bear hug—like the ones he saves for game-winning hits and diving plays in the outfield that really count.

"Yes!" I say to myself as I prance towards the infield dirt and a trip back to the bigs. "I'm on my way back. Finally. I'm out of

the bush league bandbox. Back to the Show." I gloat and give a thumbs up to my Jamaican friend. "They probably want me to pitch this weekend against the Giants. I always pitched great in Candlestick."

****

Most days in baseball come with a profound sense of foreboding—a far-off drum pounding in your ear. The pressure to win is profound. Day in, day out, it's a gut punch mixed with passion and pressure. "Play at your peak ability all the time." The voices say, "Make tons of money and live up to everyone's expectations . . . Don't embarrass yourself or the other guys wearing your colors."

Once inside Felipe's office, his voice seemed strained, strange considering I was so sure that he would be thrilled for me. His body language was anything but reassuring. The conversation was taking a turn I was not expecting. The words didn't register at first. I think I heard the word "released" spoken somewhere along the way. "You're being released tonight before the game to make room for some kid from Modesto," said Felipe. "I can't explain it. It has something to do with the impending strike. It's their decision. I'm sorry, but you need to get your stuff cleared out of the locker and go up to see the general manager for the paperwork."

I couldn't believe my ears.

"Oh yeah," Felipe added as I staggered back into the door. "Turn in your uniform. We need to change the name by game time." Softly delivered, these words arrived as body blows.

Strike three. I was out. In the blink of an eye, my baseball career was over.

****

Baseball is home to a colorful cast of characters and demonic lore, occasioned by mischievous bit players like little people in the batter's box and mules in the visiting hotel lobbies. I came to know many of them by their field names, the nicknames only teammates know, and in doing so, I grew to love the sheer joy of a high-five on a Chicago afternoon as well as the emptiness of a Baltimore hotel room after a loss.

In and out of the clubhouse, the lives of the players I met were interwoven in intensely complicated ways. Over the years, I came to understand the complexity that comes from lives that overlapped in such a dependent way. Today, at times, my memory strains to embrace individual faces and games, but I am increasingly aware that just the playing of the game was reason enough for me. The players together, and alone, were participants chosen by a game and strung together over time into a story like the well-worn leather in an old glove.

For me, the seduction of the game caught me at an early age and remained strong and undeniable. As a boy of six, I stared at the murals in my small bedroom. I was captivated by a life-size sinister-looking Ty Cobb, bearing down on third base, spikes high. He seemed to be sliding into my outstretched glove. I spent years at night tagging him out. With the help of my imagination, I could see myself in these pictures—hat peaked at the brim like Honus Wagner, hips swaggering like Willie Mays making his signature basket catch, uniform fitting loose like Ted Williams's, and always a smile for the television interview cameras after the game was over.

Ultimately the images from my childhood just could not be denied, and I would pursue my career as a professional ballplayer. Frame by frame the images piled up like old bubble gum cards in the attic. It was as if I was able to take an imprint of the images and take them with me and piece them together into a continuous full-length movie, a career—a long one, in fact, of almost eighteen years in professional ball. And although the ending could never have been scripted, I knew from an early age that I would be part of the cast. I could see the life ahead clearly, deliberately.

My view of baseball continues to be hard to pin down and harder to describe to others in any meaningful way. The truth is, the vision I had for myself grew more dimensional over time and ultimately became real. It became who I became—never quite safely ensconced and never quite willing to let go.

Today, I can still see events that transpired over thirty years ago as clearly as the day they happened. I sometimes find myself laughing out loud at a story that pops into my mind for no reason or swabbing beads of sweat from my forehead as I remember a bases-loaded situation. It's hard for me to recognize myself as that young boy who left home at the age of seventeen and never returned. After all, the man in the mirror has aged, but the insight is ageless.

EPILOGUE:
FENWAY PARK'S
CENTENNIAL
CELEBRATION AND PLAYER
REUNION, 2012

BEHIND THE CENTER field bleachers, across the street from Fenway Park in a largely abandoned old high school, an odd paradox was about to play out, involving the elite of what has been called our National Pastime and one very old venerable piece of real estate. In a few hours a celebration would commence, a birthday party for a baseball field, one into which, over the years, an entire city had breathed life into, a field of dreams, the scene of timeless contests, and a field ingrained in the memory of all who passed through its gates. Today it was to be honored with a hundred-year birthday party.

To honor the field, former players were invited to reunite in remembrance of times and things past and present.

The old building, cleaned and swept within an inch of its life, was the site of the gathering for some of the legends of baseball—men who were considered, by this city and this ballpark, nothing short of royalty. They were men who, by the mere wearing of a uniform jersey with "Red Sox" on the front, were now and forever considered part of the family. Some of these players were heroes here in Boston. Some were wealthy beyond imagination, while others were one bounced check away from bankruptcy. All were thrilled to be participants. Each reveled in his own individual and collective memories.

Two hundred and thirteen Red Sox alumni, many sporting white hair (in the cases where there was any hair at all), creeping out from behind golf hats, cowboy hats, and toupees, gathered together. They sat sucking in their beer guts as best they could, milling around folding chairs and lunchroom tables like school children, chewing on chicken tenders, and reconnecting with other players with whom they had long since lost touch. The oxygen in the room was being sucked in and spewed out in volumes of vapor and irreverence.

The room filled up slowly. Players from the last one hundred years trickled in with a mixture of surprise and expectation. Everyone here had stories, albeit different ones. Nevertheless, they all belonged.

None of the players who enter the game of baseball would escape unchanged. Their lives today had meaning beyond statistics, titles, and position. They were remembered because they were Red Sox players once, and for one more time, they reunited with friends and combatants long unremembered to honor the 100th anniversary of a remarkable field, the hallowed ground on which they played.

In celebration of Fenway's 100th anniversary, they were, one by one, going to be announced by the public address and marched out onto Fenway Park, a field of enormous importance to all Bostonians and of personal consequence to everyone in this room.

My feelings were mixed. I had played what, most would say, was a long career, eighteen years. I had played extremely well at times, but my career lacked consistency. I never played for a championship team, and my tenure was cut short way too soon by an injury that the team doctor could never correctly diagnose let alone repair. Fenway was the last field on which I had stepped thirty-two years ago, and I ardently vowed, at the time for very personal reasons, I would never step foot there again. But here I was, mouthing old game stories to other players, trying to remember names and where we played together. Crazy stories grew more outrageous, but it didn't matter, because nobody was able to validate a single detail.

We were loaded on to three city buses outside the front door of an old school and driven one hundred yards to the center field entrance of Fenway Park on Lansdowne Street. Piling off, we were ushered through an appreciative crowd, barely being contained by a two-row-deep honor guard of Massachusetts State troopers, and through the portico leading to the storage area in center field. Once inside, we lined up in a very sloppy single file.

The old corrugated garage door was rolled back, complaining, hissing, and squeaking into a ball with the help of one-hundred-year-old chain pulleys. A cold chill wafted over me.

I squinted down, looking past Nomar Garciaparra and Jeremy Remy, who were laughing about something I couldn't hear and probably wouldn't understand, down through the ambient light of the old familiar tunnel into the sunlight blazing down on the other side. I could see the grass of center field and hear the roar of the crowd going up and down like a heartbeat as the names of the players were announced. Leon Uris once wrote, "One girds for battle with fear and fantasy." I'm reminded of both as I slip the uniform shirt on again, number and name correct, for the first time in thirty-two years.

Turning one-hundred years old is no easy accomplishment. Fenway Park is an institution with its own appeal and its own history. The official Fenway Park Tour, published as a collectors' item in 2012, says Fenway "never gets old," but in the years preceding the new owners group headed by John Henry, Tom Werner, and Larry Lucchino, it had begun to show a little age.

All the players who played here know that Fenway Park is a living thing. My first steps onto Fenway field were as a fifteen-year-old high-schooler in an All New England Tournament, where the best players from all over the Northeast were brought into play a game as a showcase for tomorrow's stars. Fifty years later, there I was, retracing those steps in the spotlight with a field full of yesterday's legends.

For this special occasion, the Red Sox invited over six hundred former players. Everyone and anybody who wore the uniform, even for a day, over the one-hundred-year history of Fenway was invited to come back to the Park, be introduced to the crowd, and stand shoulder to shoulder on the field. Some came from Japan, others from Puerto Rico and the Dominican Republic. When the last person was introduced, 213 former players stood on the field milling around their former positions. These were the men who, without the job security of a multiyear contract, risked their career every single at-bat for a chance to wear the uniform.

Pulling into the player's parking lot on Yawkey Way earlier that day, I drove by the Jersey barriers and mounted cops styling in a 2000 Cadillac Coupe de Ville with 154,000 miles on it, milk-white and showing some rust. It had been my father's pride and joy before he died. My children refused to ride with me when I had the car, and I used to embarrass them picking them up at soccer practice. They said I was driving an old couch. But it was paid for, and the lot crew knew it. I looked around to make sure it was kept a safe distance from the Lamborghini and the SUV with the cable dish on the roof. It occurred to me that there had been a significant swing in the fortunes of the players from the pre-free agency days to the present.

I flashed back to the scene in Milwaukee in 1972. I was playing for the Milwaukee Brewers. Nightly attendance was around twelve thousand. One of the minority owners of the Brewers had an AMC car dealership and, in exchange for the free publicity appearances, a handful of players were offered an AMC Gremlin to use during the season. Mine was dark blue, and the generosity was greatly appreciated as there was no way I could have afforded a new car on my own. My salary at the time was comparable to that of most of my Milwaukee teammates, $12,000 for the season.

Back in the shadows underneath the centerfield stands we were standing in a three-abreast formation, a phalanx of Red Sox jerseys. I was standing tall, intentionally arching my back to the point of pain in a feeble attempt at better posture, directly behind and being pushed into Sox excoriated manager Terry Francona. Tito, as he was called by his teammates, was "holding court" and sharing a hilarious story with Kevin Millar and Pedro Martinez two rows over, completely disrupting any semblance we had of a line formation.

Terry suddenly turned to me and asked, "Skippy. When was the last time you were on this field?" He looked at me with the same mischievous eyes that had stared down the Boston press after two losing seasons. It was then that he summoned what some would say was more relief than melancholy, as he thanked the Boston fans and players three months earlier on the day he was fired from the manager's position by a team with a short memory in a city that demands a winning performance.

I had known Terry since he was an eleven-year-old boy, son of major leaguer John "Tito" Patsy Francona, a journeyman spray-hitting infielder with the Milwaukee Brewers in 1970. Our lives connected again ten years later, when I was trying in vain to make a comeback from a nagging arm injury on Montreal's AAA team in Denver, Colorado. Even though we were teammates, Terry couldn't divest himself of the recognition that I was his father's age. One of the first days he was there he called me "Sir" in the locker room, and I bent over close to his ear so no one else could hear as I said, "You call me 'sir' again, I'm going to punch you in the face." Terry only laughed and said "Yes, Sir."

Across the aisle, I could hear the raucous laughter of Bill Lee, the iconic off the wall left-hander who is still pitching competitively in professional baseball. Bill is a coat with many colors to be sure, inspiring for the sheer volume of his interminable energy. Bill and I first met in 1970 in winter ball. Both of us were young in our careers and were playing much more for the love of the game than for our meager paycheck.

Richie Hebner, a fellow Norwood, Massachusetts, Little League tryout and New York Mets teammate was in the row to my right. Hebner was busy negotiating for a beer with one of the fans who was hanging over the railing begging for autographs.

We were moving in snakelike fashion, slithering down the slightly inclined ramp towards the garage door. I turned to Terry, full-face for a fleeting few seconds before we would be separated again forever, finding a way back to his original question.

"It was 1980," I said, my eyes looking up at rusted beams of the center field storage area, capturing a fleeting image of a bedraggled uniform with my number on it. "I think these same people were booing at the time," I added in a stage whisper.

"Yeah," he said. "Tell me about it."

As the line started moving again, I began inching forward, down the ramp towards the outfield grass. On cue from the organizer with a clipboard and microphone, I stumbled forward onto the cinder surface. Hearing my name announced and seeing my name on the Jumbotron, I felt confused and disoriented by of the shards of light. The searing crowd-roar slapped across my face. Hatless, the skin on my now shiny head baked in the sun's rays, I raised my hand to protect my exposed scalp—an involuntary salute. Shortening my steps, pivoting left and right, I waved toward the loudest cheers.

I was struck by the easy way the players came together. We were sharing something in which outsiders could never be included—a silent acknowledgment of something very special, more valuable than the rings and the fancy cars. I tried to put my finger on it. At this point in time, there were certainly a lot more notable differences than similarities, but we all shared so many untold stories. Each player now in uniform had his own version of the truth and the poorly remembered facts to back it up.

John Updike completed an essay about Ted Williams by saying, "The crowd and Ted always shared what was important . . . a belief that this game terribly mattered." So I will complete this by saying: The same things that matter and make the game great, make the players focus on what really matters, keeping the love of the game in sight.

*For the young boy holding tight onto that old stick and holding as
    tightly to his dreams.*

*The unproven rookie who has the audacity to believe that his
    dreams might be true.*

*The minor leaguer standing alone, confused in the cornfields in
    Iowa*

Coming face to face with legend and heroes.

*The veteran player, trying to make a change from infielder to
    pitcher,*

Looking for a way to hang on to his dreams.

I answer that I am these people and that there's magic everywhere.

It's only the difference between what you can see and can't see,

What you believe and don't believe.

*My actions on the field turned out to be nothing more than dreams
    believed.*

Baseball connects the dreamer and the dream

Part hope . . . part real . . . part magic.

Skip Lockwood

INDEX